From Gethsemane to Pentecost

From Gethsemane to Pentecost

A Passion Study

ELIZABETH DANNA

WIPF & STOCK · Eugene, Oregon

FROM GETHSEMANE TO PENTECOST
A Passion Study

Copyright © 2011 Elizabeth Danna. All rights reserved. Except for brief quotations in critical publications or reviews, no part of this book may be reproduced in any manner without prior written permission from the publisher. Write: Permissions, Wipf and Stock Publishers, 199 W. 8th Ave., Suite 3, Eugene, OR 97401.

Wipf & Stock
An Imprint of Wipf and Stock Publishers
199 W. 8th Ave., Suite 3
Eugene, OR 97401
www.wipfandstock.com

ISBN 13: 978-1-60899-835-7

Manufactured in the U.S.A.

Unless otherwise indicated, all Scripture quotations are taken from the Revised Standard Version of the Bible, copyright 1952,[2nd edition, 1971] by the Division of Christian Education of the National Council of Churches of Christ in the United States of America. Used by permission. All rights reserved.

New Revised Standard Version Bible, copyright 1989, Division of Christian Education of the National Council of Churches of Christ in the United States of America. Used by permission. All rights reserved.

Scripture quotations marked (NIV) are taken from the Holy Bible, are taken from the Holy Bible, New International Version®, NIV®. Copyright ©1973, 1978, 1984 by Biblica, Inc.™ Used by permission of Zondervan. All rights reserved worldwide.

Contents

Acknowledgments vii
How to Use This Book ix

Week 1   Introduction 1

Week 2   Second Garden, Second Adam 6

Week 3   Jesus (and Peter) on Trial 30

Week 4   A Roman Tragedy 51

Week 5   Via Dolorosa 74

Week 6   Sealed in a Stone-Cold Tomb 94

Week 7   A Happy Beginning 113

Week 8   Wind and Fire 136

Bibliography 155

Acknowledgments

There are several people who have helped me in preparing this book, and I would like to thank them for their support. I went through an earlier version of this study with the women's Bible study group at Shoreacres Bible Chapel, Burlington, Ontario, and their input, prayers, and encouragement are much appreciated. The Rev. Charmain Sebestyen, The South Gate Presbyterian Church, Hamilton, Ontario, has been an invaluable support during this and much more through more than thirty years of friendship. I would also like to thank Christian Amondson, Jim Tedrick, and the staff at Wipf & Stock for their patience and help to a first-time author during the publication process. Above all, to God be thanks and praise.

How to Use This Book

Greetings, Friend, in the name of our crucified and risen Savior, Jesus Christ. Thank you for choosing *From Gethsemane to Pentecost*. I am glad that you are coming with me on this journey through the Gospel Passion narratives. Before we start, a few words of explanation about how this study works.

From Gethsemane to Pentecost is an eight-week study designed for small Bible study groups meeting once a week. It is also suitable for individual study. Week One is an Introduction, providing an overview of the entire study. In Week Two we begin our study of the biblical text. Each week's lesson is divided into five sections, Days One through Five (the lessons, and the days, are not all the same length). On Day One we will read the passage which we will be studying all that week, to get an overview. On days Two through Five we will reread the short passage which we will focus on that day. Each day's reading includes two questions for the group to take up when it meets, or for individual reflection. Feel free to discuss the other material as well. I have used the Revised Standard Version of the Bible throughout this study, except where otherwise indicated. You may use any version you wish. We will touch on a variety of subjects, including literary/characterization issues (that is, how the Gospel writers, as inspired storytellers, tell their stories), history, archaeology, and reasons to believe in the accuracy of the Gospel records and the reasonableness of Easter faith. We will also ask how we can apply what we learn from each passage to our own lives. Above all, my prayer is that through this study we can grow spiritually, and also come to a fresh appreciation of what Jesus did for us that first Passiontide.

WEEK 1

Introduction

THE STORY OF JESUS' death and resurrection formed the heart of Christian preaching from the earliest days of the church. Indeed the apostle Paul tells the Corinthians, "I decided to know nothing among you except Jesus Christ, and him crucified" (1 Cor 2:2). And again, "I handed on to you as *of first importance* what I in turn had received: that Christ died for your sins in accordance with the Scriptures, and that he was buried, and that he was raised on the third day in accordance with the Scriptures . . ." (1 Cor 15:3–4, emphasis added). And a saying of Jesus hints that the Passion is the reason Jesus came to earth ("For this reason I came to this hour," John 12:27). It is probable, then, that this part of the story of Jesus was the first to be formed into a coherent narrative. Indeed one scholar has described the Gospels as Passion narratives with extended introductions. By the way, the events of Jesus' suffering and death are called the "Passion" from the Latin *passio*, "suffering" (the story was given this name when Latin was the only language of the church. Indeed the Roman Catholic Church to this day lays much emphasis on the physical suffering of Jesus during his trials and crucifixion).

It was not long before Christians wanted to know more about what Jesus had said and done during his lifetime, before his crucifixion. They also found themselves faced with questions from opponents: what had Jesus done that the authorities wanted him dead? If he truly was the Messiah of God, why had God allowed him to die? To answer these questions, they did two things. First, as they told the story of Jesus they showed that he was innocent of the charges brought against him, and also that he knew ahead of time what was going to happen, and accepted it. Second, they searched the Scriptures to show that the prophets had foretold the events of Jesus' life. This was the only way they could persuade Jews to believe in Jesus, for, the Jews reasoned, God would not do anything as important as this without telling Israel beforehand (see Amos 3:7, "Surely the Lord GOD does nothing, without revealing his secret to his servants the prophets"). Mark shows in the first half of his Gospel that Jesus was able to teach, preach, cast out demons and do miracles because he was sent from God and had God's approval. When reading about Jesus' suffering and death, the reader is to understand that his dying in this way did not mean that God had rejected him (compare Acts 2:22–24, "Jesus of Nazareth, a man attested to you by God with mighty works and signs and wonders which God did through him in your midst, as you yourselves know—this Jesus, delivered up according to the definite plan and foreknowledge of God, you crucified and killed by the hands of lawless men. But God raised him up").

So why should we study the Passion story today? What value does it have for us? The first thing we may say is that the story concerns the death of Jesus, and the death of Jesus is still the only way to salvation. Jesus said, "I am the way, and the truth, and the life; no one comes to the Father, but by me" (John 14:6). "There is salvation in no one else, for there is no other name under heaven given among men by which we must be saved" (Acts 4:12). This is still true today. This alone would make this story worthy of our attention. But there is also much to be learned from these passages, and many lessons that we can apply to our own lives. Paul, writing about some tragic incidents in Israel's past, says, "These things were written down for our instruction" (1 Cor 10:11). Paul is referring to the Old Testament Scriptures, but the same thing also applies to the New Testament for us. So there are good reasons for studying these passages.

Most Bible scholars today agree on the following timeline: Jesus was crucified in about AD 30. Paul wrote his letters between about AD 50 and 67. The Gospel of Mark was written about AD 65, the Gospels of Matthew and Luke, and the book of Acts, in the 70s, and the Gospel of John in the 80s. This means that the New Testament records of Jesus' life, death, and resurrection were written within fifty years of the events themselves. This means that there would still be people alive when the Gospels were written who had been alive in Jesus' lifetime, and could confirm or refute what the church said (by way of comparison, less time elapsed between the death of Jesus and the writing of the Gospels than has elapsed between World War Two and the writing of this study. There are those who have tried to deny that the Holocaust occurred, but they have had little success, because there are still witnesses alive to refute them). This speaks in favor of the accuracy of the Gospel records.

Let us turn now to the Gospel of Mark. I have chosen to focus on Mark's Passion narrative because Mark is the shortest and earliest of the Gospels (though we will be bringing in the other Passion narratives, as well as other Scripture, as needed). Mark's Gospel was probably written around AD 65, probably at Rome. In the summer of 64 there was a terrible fire at Rome, a fire in which three of the city's fourteen wards were completely destroyed and seven more were badly damaged. Roman historians said that the fire was ordered by the emperor Nero; today's historians are more inclined to think that it started by accident. However that may be, blame for the disaster soon fell upon the Christians; the fact that at this time they were an underground Jewish sect about which the general public knew little made this all the easier. Severe persecution of Christians ensued, but was limited to the area of the city. According to church tradition, the apostles Peter and Paul were among the victims of this persecution. It was in these circumstances that Mark, Peter's assistant, was led by God to write down what he remembered Peter saying about Jesus' life, ministry and death. Mark tells his story in a way that encourages his readers to face trials with the same resolute and courageous submission to the will of God that Jesus showed when he was falsely accused by the authorities, and abandoned by his disciples and (apparently) by God. The disciples fail (at least in the short term), the reader may fail too but there is hope of restoration, and if he or she endures, God will vindicate him or her just as he vindicated Jesus. (The other Gospel writers, writing over the following two decades, in different locations and circumstances, have slightly different emphases. Luke, for example, stresses that Jesus was at peace throughout his trials because he knew that God was in charge and was with him. And John stresses Jesus' control over events and his triumphant completion of his mission. But they are all telling the same story.)

One thing that we will discuss in this study is literary and characterization issues. These concern how the Gospel writers tell their stories. I should make it clear that in discussing these things I am not suggesting that the Gospels are fiction—some stories are true stories. But God led the Gospel writers to tell their stories in such a way as to bring out certain points, according to what the church, in the time and place in which a particular Gospel was written, needed to hear.

One literary device that we will see Mark use in his storytelling is irony, an irony rooted in the fact that Jesus is not the kind of Messiah that people expected. He is not a glorious conquering military Messiah, but a Suffering Servant. No one can understand Jesus until they understand that he must suffer. John uses a similar form of irony, in which characters say more than they know. Caiaphas, for example, says more than he knows in John 11:50, "it is expedient for you that one man should die for the people, and that the whole nation should not perish." He means that it is politically expedient for one man to die, if that will avoid a Roman crackdown which would cost many lives. But as John explains in verses 51–52, the meaning of the high priest's words is that Jesus will die for the Jewish nation and the world. This kind of irony encourages the reader to come alongside the writer (often against the characters) because the reader is expected to "get it," even when the characters do not.

We will also see in these next weeks that Scripture is fulfilled. Now, "Scripture is fulfilled" is an expression that Christians use frequently—but what exactly does it mean? Perhaps the simplest thing that we may say is that certain Old Testament Scriptures, whatever meaning they had in the situation in which they were first given, also described events in the life of Jesus. An example of this is in Matt 2:15, where Matthew quotes Hos 11:1, "Out of Egypt I have called my son." In the original context, Hosea is referring to Israel's exodus from Egypt (Israel is also called God's son in Exod 4:22; compare Deut 32:18; Jer 3:19) But Matthew sees Hosea's statement as referring also to Jesus, Son of God, and his return from Egypt after the death of Herod the Great. A more famous example of this is in Isa 61:1–4. In one sense Isaiah is talking about God's call on his own life. But in another sense he is talking about Jesus, as Jesus himself makes clear (Luke 4:18–21). We saw above that showing how Jesus fulfils prophecy was an important element in the early church's witnessing to Jews.

Another thing that we will see in these next weeks is the "divine passive." Simply put, this is a way of phrasing that, instead of saying, "God did this," says, "This was done." For example, in Mark 4:24–25

Jesus warns, "the measure you give will be the measure you get, and still more will be given you. For to him who has will more be given; and from him who has not, even what he has will be taken away." By using passive verbs ("be given; be taken"), Jesus hints that it is God who will be doing the measuring, giving, and taking. This was a Jewish custom, which arose shortly before Jesus' time, to avoid unintentional irreverent use of God's name.

God led each of the Evangelists—the Gospel writers—to draw lessons from the events of Jesus' death and resurrection that God wanted Christians of the first century to apply to their lives. Let us, as part of the modern-day church, look into these things and see what we can learn from them, and how we can apply these lessons to our own lives. And let us be doers of the Word, not hearers only who deceive ourselves.

Week 2

Second Garden, Second Adam

DAY ONE

Tempted, Just As We Are
Today's key verses: Mark 14:32–52;
Luke 22:50–52; Matt 27:52–53

This week we begin our study at the beginning of the Passion narrative, in the Garden of Gethsemane. The garden was a grove of olive trees, probably on the lower slopes of the Mount of Olives, on the Kidron side, probably adjacent to an olive press (the word Gethsemane means "oil press"). The Mount of Olives is a significant location in Scripture. It is the setting for Jesus' last-days discourse of Mark 13. The Mount of Olives also figures in the story of 2 Sam 15:13–31, where David flees from Absalom across the Kidron valley, up the Mount of Olives, where he weeps and prays. In the Passion narrative Jesus, Son of David, comes to the Mount of Olives to pray; he is connected not with David the triumphant king, but with David in his suffering and weakness.

Please read Mark 14:32–52, the passage that we will be studying all this week. This is the story of Jesus' struggle in Gethsemane. It is unlikely that the church would invent this story, in which Jesus could seem weak, and the disciples fail. Jesus now comes face-to-face with the fact that the trial that he has known was coming is about to begin. The words for Jesus' emotions at verses 33–34 are strong; his distress shows his full humanity. The Greek word translated "greatly distressed" is *ekthambeo*. This word refers to being struck with astonishment, amazement, and terror. The word translated "troubled" is *ademoneo*; it means "to be in distress of mind." The word translated "very sorrowful" is *perilupos*. It comes from *peri*, meaning "around," and *lupe*, meaning "grief; physical or mental distress."[1] The combination suggests being surrounded by grief and distress, as if by enemies. These are strong words, and the effect produced by their being together, one after the other like an unbearably heavy chain, is even greater. When the force of these words is considered, Mark 14:33–34 could be read like this: "And he [Jesus] took with him Peter, James, and John, and began to be amazed and terror-stricken, and to be in distress of mind. And he said to them, 'My soul is surrounded by grief and distress, to the point that it is likely to kill me. Remain here and stay awake.'"

Jesus' falling to the ground (verse 35) indicates intense emotions and an urgent need for help (compare, e.g., Mark 5:22; Matt 17:6; 18:26, 29; Luke 5:12). He prepares for his ordeal by staying awake and praying. He cries out to the Father here at the beginning of the Passion narrative, just as he will cry out to him at its end (Mark 15:35, 37). Jesus begins his prayer by addressing God as Father, with all the confidence and trust of a son talking to his father, and affirming that for God all things are possible. Jesus asks that, if possible, he might avoid suffering. But he puts God's will above his own will, and above his own comfort. If doing God's will means suffering, Jesus is willing to suffer.

Jesus prays that the cup be taken away from him (Mark 14:36). In the Old Testament, the cup represents God's judgment poured out on sinners (Isa 51:17, 22; Jer 25:15–28; 49:12; 51:7; Lam 4:21; Ezek 23:31–34; Hab 2:16; Ps 75:8). Jesus knows that the full weight of this judgement is about to fall upon him, and he shudders at the thought of what that will mean. Commentator Frank Moloney says rightly that in this narrative "the reader is allowed into the inner recesses of Jesus' mind and heart, to find two things: terror and a determination to accept what God wants."[2] This determination has two ingredients: submission to God's authority and trust in God's goodness, whatever the circumstances look like. Thus Mark shows Jesus as the obedient Son who does his Father's will. This example must have been both a challenge and a comfort to Mark's first readers, as they faced persecution. And it can be like that for us as well.

1. For all the Greek definitions in this study I have used Bauer et al., *Lexicon*; Liddell et al., *Lexicon*; Kittel and Friedrich eds., *Dictionary*; Thayer, *Lexicon*; and Vine et al., *Dictionary*.

2. *Mark*, 292.

Jesus' resolute obedience to God is not without fear and trembling. But he does not allow his emotions to keep him from doing what God has called him to do. So he understands when we feel the same way, and he will help us to, in the words of Bible teacher Joyce Meyer, "do it afraid."

Jesus goes back and forth between his praying and his disciples, which shows his concern for the men who have been placed in his care. Here Jesus sets a challenging example for us. When we are in a difficult situation, it is not easy to get our minds off ourselves and serve others, as Jesus does here. But that is the best thing that we can do for ourselves. Satan enjoys distracting us from doing what God has called us to do. But we win a battle against him when we refuse to allow our circumstances to stop us from serving God and others. Let us look briefly at a few Biblical examples of this.

In the Old Testament, we can see this in some incidents that happen as the people of Israel, returning from exile in Babylonia, rebuild the walls of Jerusalem (the full story is told in the books of Ezra and Nehemiah). The Israelites have the authorization of King Artaxerxes to rebuild the temple, and Jerusalem's walls. Even so, opponents of the Israelites, led by Sanballat, Tobiah, and Geshem the Arab, try by various methods to distract the Israelites from their work, so that the Israelites will be defenceless against attack (see, e.g., Ezra 4:1-16; 5:1-17; Neh 2:19; 4:1-9; 6:1-14). But Ezra and Nehemiah refuse to allow themselves to be distracted from doing God's work. They keep their focus on God, and encourage the Israelites to do likewise (see, e.g., Ezra 4:3; 5:5; 7:27; 8:21-23; Neh 2:20; 4:9-15, 20; 6:9,11). The books of Ezra and Nehemiah do not actually mention Satan, but it does not need a huge leap of the imagination to see him behind the actions of Israel's enemies.

In the New Testament, there is a conversation between Jesus and Peter which also illustrates this. In Matt 16:21-23 Jesus tells his disciples that he must suffer and die. Peter rebukes him; perhaps Peter does not want to believe that the Rabbi he loves will suffer. Or perhaps Peter is aware that if Jesus suffers, his disciples, including Peter, will suffer too. But Jesus rebukes Peter: "Get behind me, Satan! You are a stumbling block to me; for you are not on the side of God, but of men" (Matt 16:23 NIV). Jesus calls Peter Satan because he knows that Satan is using Peter to distract him, by tempting him to complete his mission by some other way than the cross. This is what Satan tries to do at the beginning of Jesus' ministry, and Jesus rebukes Peter in terms very similar to his rebuke of Satan in Matt 4:10 (4:10: literally, "Get away from me, Satan!" 16:23: "Get behind me, Satan!"). It is ironic that Peter, whose nickname means "rock," is acting as a stumbling stone.

Another relevant incident is recounted in the book of Acts (Acts 16:16–18). Paul and his party are followed for several days by a slave girl whose owners profit from her skill at fortune-telling, because she is possessed by a spirit of divination. The words translated "spirit of divination" literally mean "spirit of the Python," i.e., a spirit associated with the famous oracle at Delphi, in northern Greece, where people came from all over the Mediterranean world to seek the advice of the god Apollo. But such practices had been forbidden by God (Lev 19:26; Deut 18:9–14; 1 Sam 15:23). So although the girl's words in Acts 16:17 are correct, they come from an ungodly source. There can be no doubt that Satan has sent her. And her words are not ineffective, because Paul is "very much annoyed" (Acts 16:18). So rather than put up with the annoyance, he casts the spirit out of her.

We must also understand that if we get our minds focused on ourselves, we are putting ourselves in the place where God should be. That is a form of idolatry! [Was this a part of the temptation of Gethsemane for Jesus? If anyone had the right to put himself in the place of God, Jesus did! But he was always careful to walk in submissive obedience to the Father (John 5:19; 8:28–29; 14:31)]. Self-focus also turns us away from God, who is the only source of the power that we need to get through difficult times. In difficulties, the flesh wants to turn inward, but we must resist this temptation. Instead, we must turn upward to God for strength and outward to others in service.

Luke in his Gethsemane narrative adds the detail of the bloody sweat (Luke 22:44). Medically, this can happen when a person is under such intense stress that tiny blood vessels in the skin rupture and the blood comes out with the sweat. (From now on I will not consider myself stressed out until I am sweating blood!). The condition is called *hematidrosis*.

1. What do these details, physical and linguistic, tell us about Jesus' state of mind?

It is quite clear that Jesus is in a state of intense mental and physical anguish. Facing the cross was no light thing for him! We must not think that because Jesus was fully divine as well as fully human, he did not experience the full range of emotions that we do. His temptation to avoid the physical and spiritual agonies of the cross was very real. But he did not give in to it. He resolved to do God's will, no matter what the cost. That is why the writer of Hebrews can say that Jesus "in every respect has been tempted as we are, yet without sin" (Heb 4:15). Because he did not sin by giving in to temptation, he is qualified to act as our High Priest, our Representative before a holy God. And because he was tempted, he understands our weaknesses. "Therefore he had to be made like his brethren in every respect, so that he might become a merciful and faithful high priest in the service of God, to make expiation for the sins of the people. For because he himself has suffered and been tempted, he is able to help those who are tempted . . . For we have not a high priest who is unable to sympathise with our weaknesses, but one who in every respect has been tempted as we are, yet without sin" (Heb 2:17–18; 4:15).

2. What does it mean to you that Jesus struggled with temptation?

Jesus knows what it is like to struggle with temptation, because he struggled with it too. So he is able to understand when we are tempted. More than that, he is able to help as well as to empathise. He always provides a way out of temptation (1 Cor 10:13), so that we can get away from it instead of giving in to it. Every time we are tempted, God provides an open door for us to escape. But it is up to us to walk through it. Sometimes the door may be a literal one—I do not know how many times I have had to leave a kitchen to escape the temptation to eat something I should not! Or the door may take the form of a friend to whom we can go for prayer and a word of encouragement that gets us through the temptation (in my years as a Prayer Partner with 100 Huntley Street, I have prayed with many people who called our Prayer Line for help at just such a moment). But God always makes sure that the door is there. All that we have to do is to walk through it. And every time we do—every time we make the right choice instead of the wrong one—it gets easier to make the right choice the next time temptation comes our way.

DAY TWO

Flesh and Failure
Today's Key Verses: Mark 14:37–40

Yesterday we began our study by looking at Jesus' struggle with temptation. We saw his intense emotions, which give us a hint—but only a hint—of what our salvation cost him. Please reread Mark 14:37–40, the verses that we will be focusing on today. Mark summarises the rest of Jesus' prayer vigil, which must have lasted for some time. The emphasis in these verses is not on Jesus' prayer but on the disciples' failure. Mark says that Jesus prays "saying the same words" (verse 39); in other words, he continues to ask that the cup be taken away from him. There are those who say that the church must have invented the content of Jesus' prayers, because the disciples could not have heard what he actually said if they were sleeping. But there is no reason to believe that they fell asleep so quickly that they did not hear anything of what Jesus said.

Matt 26:42 says, "Again, for the second time, he [Jesus] went away and prayed, 'My Father, if this cannot pass unless I drink it, thy will be done.'" Jesus' second prayer ends, "Your will be done." Professor William Barclay[3] says that there are four ways to say, "Your will be done."

- With bitterness and resentment, as one who knows that there is no other way, but is angry about it.
- With resigned acceptance, because there is nothing to do but admit defeat by someone stronger.
- With the acceptance of one who knows that there is nothing that they can do about the situation. This is to do without a struggle what one would be forced to do anyway.
- With the calmness and joy that come from love and trust. Here is the acceptance that comes from choosing not to doubt the will of God. To choose this response is to follow the example of Jesus.

Barclay says that the real reason that we so often find it difficult to accept God's will is that at bottom we think that if only we could have things our way, we would be happy. But we must see this kind of think-

---

3. *Lord's Prayer*, 80–82.

ing for what it really is. It really means thinking that we know better than God. This is pride, and it is a very dangerous sin.

Pride was the sin of Adam and Eve when they did the one thing that God had told them not to do (Gen 3:1–24), and it will lead to our downfall as surely as it led to theirs (Prov 16:18). It is interesting that their sin took place in a garden. The pride that they showed in Eden is the opposite of the obedience that Jesus shows in the garden of Gethsemane. The first Adam's pride led him to rebel against God, but the Second Adam, Jesus, submitted to God, which led him to obey God, to the point of death (on this see Rom 5:12–19; 1 Cor 15:21–22).

Pride can also be very subtle, creeping up on us unawares and ensnaring us. It is an attitude that we can have without being aware of it until God brings it to our attention. This is why pride is so dangerous. The best way to avoid pride is to humble ourselves under God's hand, and trust that he will lift us up in due time (1 Pet 5:6). Submitting to God's will is not always easy. But it will always bring rewards—maybe not immediately, but "in due time."

We may find it easier to submit to God's will if we believe, first, in God's wisdom—that he knows what he is doing even when we do not know what he is doing, and he knows better than we do—and, second, that difficult circumstances do not mean that God does not love us. We often quote Jer 29:11, "For surely I know the plans that I have for you, says the LORD, plans for your welfare and not for harm, to give you a future with hope." But we forget that verse 11 is connected by the word "for" to verse 10: "Thus says the LORD: When seventy years are completed for Babylon, I will visit you and I will fulfil to you my promise and bring you back to this place [Jerusalem]." Notice the first part of this verse: God will visit Israel and keep his promise to her, but only after the seventy years of the Babylonian exile are completed. In other words, the pain and loss of the exile are part of God's good plan for Israel.

It is the same way in our individual lives. Trials are what God uses to build in us character which we would not develop any other way (see also Rom 5:3–5). Submitting to God's plan for us—the hard parts as well as the easy ones—is what opens the door for us to become more like Jesus, which is God's ultimate will for us (Rom 8:29). We can only achieve this kind of submissive obedience when we receive Jesus into our heart and he empowers us to achieve it. It is not something that comes naturally, only supernaturally.

In Mark 14:37–38, Mark shifts his focus from Jesus to the disciples. Their behavior is in complete contrast to the behavior of Jesus. We could say that they show us an example of what *not* to do! As I said yesterday, it is unlikely that the church would make this story up. It is so embarrassing that it would not have been told if it were not true! Under God's leading, Mark preserves it as a warning to his first readers—and to us—not to go unprepared for trouble.

Jesus tells the disciples to watch and pray, as he does, but they go to sleep instead. Jesus takes Peter, James, and John a little further than the other disciples. In Mark 10:35, 38 Jesus asks James and John if they can drink the cup which he is about to drink. In this narrative, as Jesus prays that the cup be taken from him, James and John prove not to be as able to drink it as they think they are. And Peter is not able to live up to his earlier boasting (Mark 14:29, 31) either.

3. On what other occasions has Jesus taken these three apart from the others?

Peter, James, and John formed an inner circle within the circle of the disciples, even closer to Jesus than the rest of the Twelve (one thing that indicates this is that these three are the only ones to whom Jesus gives nicknames). They have been apart with him on three previous occasions. First, there is the raising of the daughter of Jairus from the dead (Mark 5:22–43). The second occasion is the transfiguration (Mark 9:2–8), when they get a glimpse of Jesus' heavenly glory. There are several literary connections between the Gethsemane narrative and the Transfiguration narrative. First, both these stories focus on the inner circle of disciples. Second, the phrase "he took with him" appears at both Mark 9:2 and Mark 14:33. Third, at Mark 9:6 Mark says that Peter "did not know what to say;" at Mark 14:40 Mark says that the disciples "did not know what to answer him" (the two phrases are even closer in the Greek than they are in English).

The third time that these three are with Jesus, apart from the others, is in Jerusalem. When Jesus prophesies the destruction of the Jerusalem temple (Mark 13:1–2), this inner circle of disciples and Peter's brother Andrew come to him and ask about it. He replies with a discourse about the end times (Mark 13:4–37). Now again in Gethsemane he takes them further than the others. Are they expecting some special revelation, like they have received before? Previously Jesus has shown them his power and glory—here they see his weakness and distress. One scholar asks if they miss seeing something special because they do not stay alert. Or maybe Jesus wants them to understand that glory comes only through suffering, and his struggle here *is* the special revelation . . .

At the end of the end-times speech of Mark 13:4–37, Jesus says, "And what I say to you I say to all: Watch!" (verse 37, compare verse 35). And in Mark 14:37, 40 Jesus "finds them [the disciples] sleeping," while in Mark 13:36 he warns the disciples to watch out, in case the returning master of the house "finds you sleeping." These verbal connections emphasise the last-days dimensions of what is about to happen. Throughout his ministry, Jesus has been fighting against Satan and his demonic forces in the world, by exorcising demons from the possessed and healing the sick. There is a sense in which, with the coming of Jesus, the end times have begun, and this has in fact been the first round of the final battle between God and Satan. Here in the Passion this first round is about to reach its climax.

When Jesus returns to his disciples for the first time, he speaks to Peter first, before speaking to the others as well. As Peter is the most outspoken in his boasting (Mark 14:29, 31), so he is the first to receive a rebuke for failure. In Mark 14:38 Jesus tells the disciples, "Pray that you do not come into temptation." The Greek word used here for "temptation," *peirasmos,* may also be translated "the time of testing." *Peirasmos* and its related verb usually refer to testing something to see if it is genuine. Paul, for example, tells the Corinthians, "Examine yourselves, to see whether you are living in the faith" (2 Cor 13:5). And the risen Jesus says to the church in Ephesus, "You have tested those who claim to be apostles but are not, and have found them false" (Rev 2:2). God sometimes tests our faith. But he will not allow us to be tested more than we can bear (1 Cor 10:13; he may test us more than we *think* that we can bear, but that is the stretching that is part of the testing. If we think that we can bear it ourselves, we will not turn to God for strength, which is what he wants us to do). The idea is of a test which we want to pass, but we could fail.

4. What is the most likely situation in which we will fail a test?

We are most likely to fail a test if we are not ready for it. For a student in school, the way to prepare for a test is to study. Disciples of Jesus can also expect to undergo a different kind of test, tests which demand as much preparation as school exams. We prepare for these tests by spending time with our Teacher in daily prayer and Bible study, and regular church involvement. Unlike school exams, we will not know when these tests will come, only that they will come, like "pop quizzes." And if we do not prepare for them in advance, we will fail as surely as the disciples failed in Gethsemane. We can avoid this mistake by spending time regularly with God. This is how we develop the close relationship with God which we need when trials come. This is how we strengthen our spirit and guard against the weakness of the flesh.

The disciples need to pray not to enter into temptation because, quite clearly, they are not ready to deal with it. As Jesus puts it, "The spirit is willing, but the flesh is weak" (Mark 14:38). What does this famous saying mean? Jesus means that the disciples' human spirit is drawn to God, but there is still too much of the flesh in them. This makes the testing all the more dangerous, because their fleshly pride is likely to convince them they are more prepared for the trial than they actually are.

The contrast between flesh and spirit is an important one in the New Testament, especially in Paul's letters. We must understand clearly that "the flesh" is not the same as the physical body. God created the human body along with everything else that exists, and he still regards it as "very good" (Gen 1:31). The flesh is the part of human nature which rebels against God, putting its own will above the will of God. It is self-focused and self-indulgent, and resists discipline of any kind. It is the part of human nature which gives in to temptation and sin. It is often contrasted with spirit. "Spirit" here in Mark 14:38 refers to the human spirit. This is the part of human nature which is drawn to God, and responds to His love and mercy toward us. It does not refer to the Holy Spirit, which has not yet been given (we will study the giving of the Spirit in Week 8).

Earlier I mentioned the sin of Adam and Eve. Their disobedience to God infected them with sin, an infection which they passed on to all their descendants to this day. Jesus, the Second Adam, succeeded where the first Adam failed. By his submissive obedience to God, Jesus undid the catastrophic results of Adam's rebellious disobedience. Adam's sin led to condemnation for all humanity. But Jesus' righteous act provides a free gift of grace which provides acquittal for anyone who chooses to receive the gift. How thankful I am that while Adam gave in to temptation in a garden, Jesus did not!

DAY THREE

"Let Us Go"
Today's Key Verses: Mark 14:41–42

Please reread Mark 14:41–42. This is not the most active part of the Gethsemane narrative, if only because the disciples are sleeping again! But here is the narrative's turning point. Because here Jesus makes his decision to accept God's plan for Jesus to go to the cross.

When Jesus returns to the disciples for a third time, he apparently finds then sleeping again, because he asks them, "Are you still sleeping and taking your rest?" While the King James Version of the Bible punctuates this as an instruction ("Sleep on and take your rest"), it is best taken as a question (as in RSV and some other versions). The question contains a note of rebuke: *Are you really sleeping at a time like this?* But if Jesus rebukes the disciples for failing to see the significance of what is happening this evening, we will see that he does not give up on them. The heaviness of their eyes is a sign of the weakness of the flesh. They do not know what to say to Jesus because they are embarrassed by their weakness and failure.

The word translated "it is enough" in Mark 14:41 is *apechei*, and scholars have long debated as to exactly what it means here. It was the word that merchants would write across a customer's bill when payment was complete, like our "PAID" stamp. One possible meaning is, "The money has been paid"—meaning that Jesus knows that Judas has accepted money to betray him. [Thirty pieces of silver (Matt. 26:15) probably means thirty shekels, or about 120 *denarii*—less than half of the value of the oil of nard with which Jesus is anointed at Bethany (Mark 14:5), concerning which some of those present complain about the waste].

Another good possibility is that the meaning is, "the matter is settled." According to this interpretation, Jesus has made his request of the Father that the cup be taken away from him, and is waiting for an answer. At Mark 14:41 he can hear the arresting party approaching (they arrive "while he was still speaking," verse 43); this tells him that the Father has answered his request, and the answer is No. Having understood what God's will is, he goes to meet it with courage and dignity. We may compare David's attitude toward his baby's death (2 Sam 12:15–23).

During the child's illness, David fasts, mourns, and prays that God will spare the child's life. When the child dies, David washes himself, changes his clothes, and asks his servants for food. They do not understand why he stops mourning when the child dies, so he explains. Further appeals to God by fasting and praying will not bring the child back. The baby's death means that God's answer to David's request is No, and David understands that he must accept the situation. His submissive obedience in this painful situation clears the way for the next event that is recorded: the birth of the promised heir, Solomon (2 Sam 12:24–25).

All this leads me to think about how we should respond when God says No to our requests. The first thing that we must understand is that we should not be surprised when this happens. Good parents do not give their children everything that they ask for, because children sometimes ask for things that are not actually good for them. Children do not always know what is good for them. They are swayed by bright packaging, peer pressure, or what feels good rather than unpleasant. So it is up to parents to tell their children No when they ask for something that is not in the child's best interest. It is the same with our heavenly Father. Just because we are God's children, that does not guarantee that he will give us everything we ask for! Like children, we do not always recognise what is good for us and what is not. We want pleasure and comfort, forgetting that too much ease will make us fat and lazy. The saying "No pain, no gain" is as true in the spiritual realm as it is in the physical world!

But we must also understand that because our heavenly Father is good, he will give us everything we need, everything that is good for us (see, e.g., Ps 84:11; Matt 7:9–10). When God says No to our requests, we need to trust that if he does not give us what we want, it is because he has something better to give us, just as he gave Solomon to David, in place of the child born from adultery. If God does not take you away from that difficult employment situation or those bothersome neighbors, he wants to develop you into a better person than you would be otherwise. In such a situation, we need to ask God, "What do you want me to learn from this?" and to ask for grace to endure, and for a teachable spirit that will receive what God wants to teach us. If you are attracted to someone and they do not feel the same way about you, you can trust that God has someone better for you. Several years ago, I was fired from a job, with little notice and no explanation. The fact that I did not like the job and my boss was difficult to get along with did not make being fired any less painful! But eventually God led me to a job that was more congenial, with more hours, better pay, and a better boss.

The problem is that we cannot see the end of the story while we are in the middle of it. All we can see is that we have asked God for something and he has not given it to us. We cannot see how what we are asking for might not be God's best for us, or the better thing that he has to give us if we will trust him and let go of what we want. The best thing that we can do is to "trust and obey," believing that God will bring us through, and that the "after" will be better than the "before," and better than it would have been if we had not gone "through."

Let us return to the Gethsemane story. The Scriptures (Mark 14:49) and Jesus' prophecies (Mark 14:50, compare Mark 14:27) are being fulfilled, a theme we will see throughout the rest of the Passion narrative. This is why he can say, "The hour has come." Everything is in place for the great trial, Jesus knows what is about to happen and goes into it willingly. That means that whatever things may look like on the surface, Jesus' opponents, Jewish and Roman, are not as in charge of things as they think they are.

5. What is interesting about the fact that in Mark 14:42 Jesus says to the disciples, "Let us go?"

There are two notable points about this instruction. First, "go" is a verb of movement, not of staying still—and the movement is forward, not backward. Once the arresting party arrives, there can be no doubt about what will happen next, and Jesus goes to meet it with courage and resolve (this is true no matter how one interprets *apechei*). Second, the disciples have just let Jesus down, and are about to do so again, but he still calls them to share in his work, because he knows that they will rally.

In spite of their failure, Jesus refuses to give up on the disciples. He has called them (Mark 1:16-20; 2:13-14; 3:13-19) and nothing can change that (compare Rom 11:29, "the gifts and the call of God are irrevocable.)" Throughout the Gospel of Mark, the disciples repeatedly fail to understand Jesus (Mark 4:13; 6:37, 52; 8:3-4, 17-21; 9:10), show a lack of faith (Mark 4:40-41), and jockey for position among themselves [(Mark 9:34; 10:35-41)—hardly a sign of spiritual maturity! compare 1 Cor 3:1-4]. No wonder Jesus occasionally becomes exasperated with them (e.g., Mark 8:17–18). Indeed it is interesting to note that Mark, writing what he remembers Peter saying, is harder on the disciples than the other Gospel writers. It is not too difficult to imagine Peter saying to Mark, his assistant, "What a bunch of idiots we were then. We just did not get it!" But Jesus continues to work with them. (By the way, before we get too hard on the disciples, we need to ask ourselves if we would have done any better if we had been in their place. From our position, this side of Easter and the coming of the Holy Spirit, it is easy for us to see what the disciples should have understood. But we must not get prideful. Most of us, if we are honest, would have to admit that in the disciples' place, we would do no better than they did.) And from the book of Acts, and tradition preserved by the church, we know that they went on to accomplish much for God.

This is good news, because it applies to disciples of Jesus today as much as it did to those first disciples. As soon as you became a disciple of Jesus, God began a good work in you, and you can be sure that he "will complete it until the day of Christ" (Phil 1:6). Unfortunately, the work does not usually happen overnight. When I look at myself, I sometimes hope that it will not take God until the day of Christ to complete his work in me! But there is a sense in which it will take until then, because we will not be all God wants us to be until we get to heaven. Only then will his work in us be complete. If you feel you have a long way to go, do not be discouraged. God is still at work in you. He has not given up on you, so do not give up on yourself! It may help to look at how far you have come with God, instead of always focusing on how far you have to go.

In Mark 14:41 Jesus announces that he has been betrayed into the hands of sinners. We may also note how similar the phrasing of Mark 14:41 is to the Passion prediction of Mark 9:31. In Mark 9:31 Jesus says, "The Son of man will be delivered into the hands of men;" in Mark 14:41 he says, "The Son of man is betrayed into the hands of sinners." In the Greek the word translated "delivered" and "betrayed" is the same word, *paradidetai*. In other words, what Jesus predicted is coming about. Earlier at dinner, Jesus has been more specific about this. He has said that the betrayer will be one of the Twelve (Mark 14:18–20). He confirms the prophecy with a solemn "Truly, I say to you." In Mark 14:43 Judas, identified as "one of the Twelve" (compare 14:10), arrives with the arresting party. This is no surprise to the reader, who has read about how Judas goes to the to the Jewish leadership and offers to betray Jesus to them (Mark 14:10). There is no indication in the text that Jesus knows about this by natural means. Rather Mark wants the reader to understand that Jesus knows supernaturally what Judas is planning. And this is not the only prophecy of Jesus that is coming true. On the way to the Mount of Olives, Jesus says to the disciples, "You will all fall away" (Mark 14:27); in Mark 14:50 Mark says that the disciples "all forsook him [Jesus] and fled." By drawing attention like this to the accuracy of Jesus' predictions, Mark shows Jesus as the Prophet whose prophecy is accurate and therefore trustworthy. This is significant, because some of Jesus' prophecies—namely the end-times prophecy of chapter 13 and his promise to meet his disciples in Galilee after he is raised (Mark 14:28; 16:7)—will not be fulfilled until after the end of Mark's story. But the reader, having seen some of Jesus' prophecies fulfilled, is encouraged to believe that the rest of them will also be fulfilled, in due time.

But there is more. Maybe God has spoken a word to you about your own life. If so, you can be sure that what he has said will come about. "God is not man, that he should lie. Has he said, and will he not do it? Or has he spoken, and will he not fulfil it?" (Num 23:19). God has a call on your life. You can be certain he will put you in position to do what he has called you to do. "He who promised is faithful" (Heb 10:23).

It may be that you have been waiting a while for God to fulfil his word about you. Maybe it has been a long time since that promise was made. I know what that is like! Do not give up on God, or on yourself. God's timing is perfect, even when we wonder why he is taking so long. Even when you do not see anything happening, God is at work, behind the scenes and within you. It is like when we plant a seed in a garden. For a few weeks nothing seems to be happening. But underneath the ground, out of sight, the seed is sprouting and putting out roots. Finally the shoot pushes up above the ground, where it can be seen. And even then, another few weeks will go by before the flower blooms.

6. Has God made you a promise, but you had to wait for a while before he kept it? If it is appropriate, why not share with the group?

Our Biblical example here is Abraham. He was seventy-five years old when God first promised him an heir (Gen. 12:2, 4), and one hundred years old when Isaac was born (Gen. 21:5). Twenty-five years passed between the promise and the fulfillment. By human standards, that is a long time to wait! So maybe it is not surprising that Abraham had the occasional weak moment (see, e.g., Gen 15:2–3). But for the most part he trusted that God would keep his promise, and his faith was credited to him as righteousness (Gen 15:6; Heb 11:11–12). And God did keep his promise, even if it was in a way that no one expected. But I wonder if Abraham and Sarah delayed the fulfilling of the promise by "helping" God, trying to fulfil it their own way. Did they delay the coming of Isaac by taking things into their own hands and producing Ishmael? If you are waiting on God, the best thing you can do is to keep trusting him. That is not easy. But God always keeps his promises—on his schedule, not ours.

DAY FOUR

Into the Hands of Sinners
Today's Key Verses: Mark 14:43–46

Please reread Mark 14:43–46. In verse 43 the arresting party arrives. They have been sent by "the chief priests and the scribes and the elders" (i.e., the Jewish authorities). By saying that they are carrying both swords and clubs, Mark hints that there are Roman soldiers as well as Jewish temple attendants in the arresting party, because the temple attendants normally carried clubs. John makes this clear, because the words that he uses for "band of soldiers" and "captain" (John 18:3, 12) are the usual words for Roman soldiers and their commander. Judas is acting as their guide; he knows that Jesus and the disciples are in Gethsemane, because they have been there before (John 18:2). He has aligned himself with those who want to arrest Jesus, so he is "standing with them" (John 18:5) in a symbolic as well as a literal way. All Jesus' opponents—the Jewish authorities, the Romans, and the traitorous disciple—are represented here, gathered against him.

Luke 22:48 says, "But Jesus said to him, "Judas, would you betray the Son of man with a kiss?" In other words, Jesus makes a last-minute appeal to Judas to repent and change his mind: *"Are you really going to betray the Son of Man with a kiss?"* How merciful he is! Even at this moment Jesus reminds Judas that he still has options and a way of escape from his course of action (compare 1 Cor 10:13). But Judas has made his choice and will not go back on it. He identifies Jesus by a kiss. A kiss of greeting was a customary gesture between friends in that culture (compare Luke 7:45), and was also a respectful way for students to greet their rabbi. A kiss from an enemy, however, is ironic (compare Prov 27:6). But while Judas speaks like a disciple by using the title Rabbi, he is not dong what Jesus says, which is the mark of a true disciple (Luke 6:46, 48). Even as he betrays Jesus, Judas is identified as "one of the Twelve" (Mark 14:43). This is Mark's expression of grief and dismay that someone so close to Jesus could do such a thing.

7. Have you ever been betrayed? If it is appropriate, why not share your experience with the group, without mentioning any names?

Maybe you have known the pain of being betrayed by someone close to you. Someone you thought you could trust. If so, take comfort in knowing that Jesus understands how you feel (knowing that it was going to happen did not make it any less painful for him). He has known that pain too, and he is able to help you heal. Release your pain to him, put it in his hands. He knows what happened and how you were hurt. If you trust him to deal with it, he will.

Why does Judas betray Jesus? Mark does not say. But the other Gospels give us a few hints. In Matt 26:14–15 Judas asks the Jewish authorities, "What will you give me if I deliver him to you?" and they give him money. And in John 12:6 we read that Judas is a thief: he is in charge of the money box (i.e., he acts as the ministry's treasurer), and takes what has been put into it (the verb tense suggests that he has done this more than once). This suggests greed as a motive for the betrayal.

The Gospels also hint that something other than greed may be behind what Judas does. John 13:2 says, "the devil had already put it into the heart of Judas Iscariot, Simon's son, to betray him [Jesus]." And again, "after the morsel [of food], Satan entered into him" (John 13:27). We may also note that at John 17:12 Jesus refers to Judas as "the son of perdition," the same expression used for the Antichrist at 2 Thess 2:3; and at John 6:70 Jesus refers to Judas as "a devil." Luke combines the two motives. "Then Satan entered into Judas called Iscariot, who was of the number of the twelve; he went away and conferred with the chief priests and officers how he might betray him to them. And they were glad, and engaged to give him money" (Luke 22:3–5). And indeed the two motives are not mutually exclusive. In fact they are most likely connected: Judas's greed leaves him open to Satan's influence (we will talk more about Judas next week).

It is also possible that Judas wants to pressure Jesus into taking some kind of overt action to prove that he is the Messiah. Perhaps Judas wants Jesus, the Son of David, to make a claim to the throne and overthrow both Herod and the Romans (as the crowd do at John 16:15). If so, Judas has not understood what kind of Messiah Jesus is.

Jesus' response to Judas, as recorded by Matthew (Matt 26:50), is difficult to translate, but the best translation seems to be, "Friend, do what you are here for." This means that Jesus knows what Judas is up to, and is actually giving him permission to betray him! Again we see that Jesus is the one who is really in charge. His use of the word "friend" here at Matt 26:50 is ironic, and contains a note of rebuke (compare Matt 20:13; 22:12). One may also compare 2 Sam 15:37; 16:16–17, where Hushai is called David's friend. It is ironic that here the Son of David uses that word "friend" about a traitor.

The mention of David in the context of Jesus' betrayal by Judas reminds us that David was also betrayed by someone close to him—his son Absalom. Absalom's attempt to overthrow his father and usurp his throne was as painful to David as Judas' informing the authorities where Jesus could be arrested was to Jesus. But David still mourns greatly when Absalom dies (2 Sam 18:33–19:4). Similarly Jesus says, "woe to that man by whom the Son of man is betrayed! It would have been better for that man if he had never been born" (Mark 14:21). Neither Absalom nor Judas profit from what they do, because their actions lead to their deaths. Judas hangs himself from a rope (Matt 27:5), and Absalom is speared by General Joab while dangling from a tree in which his head has been caught (2 Sam 18:9, 14–15).

As I am writing this part of this study, the church is preparing not for Easter but for Christmas. It is appropriate for us to be thinking about Jesus' death even as we celebrate his birth. Because Jesus' birth would have no significance if it were not for the events of his Passion. And there are several connections between the two stories.

It is hard, for example, not to think of Christmas without thinking of Mary, Jesus' mother. What we do not always think about is how courageous this teenager was (in accordance with the custom of the time, she probably became engaged to Joseph at age twelve or thirteen). Luke does not record Mary's thought processes as the angel tells her that she has been chosen to give birth to the Son of God, or in the months afterward. Does she worry about what other people will think when they find out that she is pregnant and unmarried? Does she wonder whether Joseph will believe her when she tells him that she is pregnant by the Holy Spirit, or if he will think that she has been cheating on him (it seems that this is exactly what Joseph does think, until an angel corroborates her story; see Matt 1:18–21)? Luke records only Mary's response: "Behold, I am the handmaid of the Lord; let it be to me according to your word" (Luke 1:38). In Nazareth just before the beginning of Jesus' earthly life, Mary shows the same courageous obedience to God as Jesus shows at the end of his earthly life.

8. Has God told you to do something that will take courage? Have you asked him for the courage to obey his will? If not, why not ask the group to pray with you?

Another connection between the Christmas story and the Passion story, as Matthew tells them, concerns the Gentiles. In Matt 2:1–12, "wise men from the east" (Matt 2:1; they are probably astrologers from Parthia, now Iraq) come to Bethlehem to pay homage to Jesus. These Gentiles are quicker to acknowledge who Jesus is than the Jews, represented by Herod the Great, who wants to kill Jesus (Matt 2:13–18). Similarly in Matthew's Passion narrative, Pilate tries to release Jesus (Matt 27:18–26), and his wife recognises Jesus as an innocent man (Matt 27:19), while the Jewish authorities push for his crucifixion (we will talk more about Pilate, and his wife, in Week 4).

Returning to the Gospel of Mark, it is at this point that the arresting party actually takes Jesus into custody. Mark's narration of such a pivotal moment is brief: "they laid their hands on him and seized him" (Mark 14:46). Such brevity is the usual style of the New Testament Gospel writers, who focus on what is important and avoid unnecessary details. So far we have seen a lot of preparing, thinking and choosing (or the lack thereof); tomorrow we will see some action!

DAY FIVE

Fight and Flight
Today's Key Verses: Mark 14:47–52;
Luke 22:50–52; Matt 26:52–53

Today we come to the end of the Gethsemane story; please reread Mark 14:47–52. This is the part of the story that has the most action, as the disciples react to Jesus' arrest, and the arresting party fight back. But all the action flows from Jesus' earlier choice to accept God's will.

If Jesus is willing to allow himself to be arrested, his disciples have other ideas. One of them (John says that it is the ever-impetuous Peter; John 18:10) goes so far as to cut off the ear of the high priest's servant (I suspect that he is actually trying to cut the man's throat, or cut off his head!). It is interesting that Mark uses the phrase "those who stood by." Moloney says,

> This is a deliberate and subtle change of direction on the part of the storyteller, as those who have been known throughout the Gospel as "the disciples" . . . approach their final appearance in the story (v. 50), they are no longer regarded as "disciples." Their failure to learn from the ways and word of Jesus relegates them to the position of "those who stood by."[4]

In other words, Mark does not call them disciples here because they are not acting like disciples.

Please reread Luke 22:50–52. The disciple's *striking* the servant contradicts Jesus' prophecy (Mark 14:27) that Jesus will be the one who is struck, in fulfilment of Zech 13:7. But no human effort can prevent Jesus' prophecies from being fulfilled. Luke says that Jesus heals the ear (thus allowing the servant to return to temple service) before protesting to the arresting party that they are treating him like a bandit although he is no such thing. In Mark 11:17 Jesus says that the Jewish authorities have made the temple "a den of robbers," in effect calling them robbers. Here they are acting as if Jesus is the robber.

---

4. *Mark*, 297.

9. What is significant about the order in which Jesus does things here?

We must note that Jesus expresses his love for his opponents (by healing the ear) before he rebukes them for their sin. Here again Jesus provides an important example for us. There is a place for challenging people about their sin, and calling on them to repent and turn away from it. But before we do that, we must show them that God loves them and we love them. Otherwise our calls for repentance sound unloving and judgemental, and people will react by rejecting them rather than responding with repentance. I am not talking about the idea that we must feed hungry people before we can preach to them. In some parts of the world, to feed all the hungry is too big a task for any one person. I am talking about the impression we give to the people we interact with every day. We are not going to win our unbelieving relatives, neighbours or co-workers to Christ if we act holier-than-thou with them or sit in judgment on them. We must speak the truth, but we must do it in love (Eph 4:15), out of genuine concern for the sinner's welfare rather than to score points over them with others or make ourselves feel better. Before we speak out, we must ask ourselves about our motives for speaking. If we are going to correct someone, we must do it with humility, knowing that we could be the next to stumble unless God in his mercy keeps us from stumbling (Gal 6:1).

10. What effect does Jesus' healing of the ear have on the arresting party? On the disciples?

Jesus' action of healing seems to have no effect on either group—it is as if no one notices what Jesus does, at least not at that moment. What effect it has on the high priest's servant—who can hardly fail to notice what Jesus does for him—is not said. Mark does not mention the servant's name, or what he does in the temple. But Mark calls him *the* servant of the high priest (not *a* servant). This indicates that he is a senior official who has probably dedicated his life to temple service. Does he feel relief that he will not be excluded from temple service because of a mutilated ear (see Lev 21:17–18)? Does he feel guilt or shame as he arrests the man who has done this for him? We are not told. But we can say that Jesus' action has no effect on what the high priest's servant does.

Everyone else is focused on what *they* are doing rather than what Jesus is doing. This makes me wonder how often we miss God's action because we are caught up in our circumstances. We can get so focused on what is happening to us, and how we feel about it, and what we want to happen, that we can miss what God does for us. This is especially true if we are expecting him to intervene in one particular way (we can be certain that no one was expecting Jesus to heal the servant's ear). We need to expect the unexpected from God, and avoid thinking that God can deal with our situations only in the way we think that he should deal with them.

Our Biblical example here is John 11:1–44, the raising of Lazarus. When Martha and Mary send for Jesus, they are probably expecting him to come and heal Lazarus. This is why both sisters say, "Lord, if you had been here, my brother would not have died" (John 11:21, 32). It is unlikely that they are expecting him to wait in Perea until Lazarus dies, then come and raise Lazarus from the dead! But by doing things his way, Jesus gets more glory for himself, and gives more glory to God, than if he had done things the way Martha and Mary wanted him to (see John 11:42).

We must also be careful to keep our focus on God, not on our circumstances or our emotions. Our example in this is Peter's walking on water (Matt 14:29–31). As long as Peter keeps his eyes on Jesus, he is able to walk on water. But when he sees the wind (i.e., when he gets his eyes onto his circumstances), he panics, doubts, and starts to sink. But Jesus is there to catch him. We can be deceived by our circumstances, but God will never deceive us.

Let us return to the Gethsemane story; please reread Matt 26:52–53. Jesus responds to his disciple's violence by pointing out, first, that those who take up the sword will die by the sword. This saying is perhaps to be connected with his earlier sayings, that his disciples must not return evil for evil, but must love their enemies (Matt 5:38–48). Second, he reminds them that if he wanted help, he could ask for it, and his Father would send a legion of angels each for himself and the eleven remaining disciples. [Note that Jesus has already refused to call for angelic assistance, when Satan tempted him to do so (Matt 4:6)]. Since a legion numbered anywhere from 3,000 to 6,000 soldiers, twelve legions is a rather large army!

What the disciples do not realize, or do not want to accept, is that to follow Jesus is likely to mean following him in suffering and death. Jesus has called them to join him with "Let us go" (Mark 14:42). But that does not mean that he is calling them to ease and safety: "See, my betrayer is at hand." In saying this, Jesus calls them to share his suffering.

But the news is not all bad. Earlier, Jesus has said, "If any one serves me, he must follow me, and where I am, there shall my servant be also; if any one serves me, the Father will honour him" (John 12:26). In the context of John 12, being where Jesus is means being with him in suffering and death (John 12:24–25, 27, 33). But the last part of verse 25 and the last part of verse 26 suggest that those who suffer with Jesus will be rewarded. As Paul says, "The saying is sure: If we have died with him, we shall also live with him; If we endure, we shall also reign with him" (2 Tim 2:11–12).

Jesus is prepared to submit to what is ahead of him, because he knows that this is how the Scriptures will be fulfilled. The disciples, on the other hand, abandon their Master and run. Jesus' prophecy in Mark 14:27 ("You will all fall away; for it is written, 'I will strike the shepherd, and the sheep will be scattered;'" compare Zech 13:7) is coming true. In the Greek of Mark 14:50, Mark emphasises the word for "deserted" by putting it first, and the word for "all" by putting it last. In this way he focuses on how complete the disciples' failure is. There is an irony here, because at Mark 1:18–20 the fishermen leave their nets when Jesus calls them; but at Mark 14:50 they leave Jesus. They fail because they have not learned to follow Jesus by denying themselves and taking up their cross. In Mark 10:28–30, Peter says that they have left everything to follow Jesus, for which Jesus promises rewards. In leaving Jesus in Gethsemane, they abandon (however temporarily) the destiny that he has called them to, and so they lose an opportunity to serve God by serving Jesus. They illustrate the choice Jesus lays out in Mark 8:35–37. "For whoever would save his life will lose it; and whoever loses his life for my sake and the gospel's will save it. For what does it profit a man, to gain the whole world and forfeit his life? For what can a man give in return for his life?"

One possible explanation for the disciples' failure is that they may simply be tired or stressed. Mark does not specifically say this, though the mention of heavy eyes (Mark 14:40) may hint at it. And Luke says that when Jesus returns to the disciples for the last time, he finds them "sleeping for sorrow" (Luke 22:45). If the disciples have any idea of what is coming that night and the next day, it would be understandable if they are frightened. The resulting stress and weariness leave them unable to stand in the face of danger.

We also must be aware of this. Stress and fatigue can leave us open to depression, discouragement, and attack from the enemy. There are several things that we can do to prevent this from happening. First, we can maintain a close relationship with God through prayer, Bible study and church involvement. Second, we can guard against fatigue by making sure that we get enough rest, relaxation, and sleep. This may mean delegating some things to others, and telling people that we are too busy to take on anything else. Third, we can guard against stress by casting our cares on God (1 Pet 5:7). Whatever our concerns are, he is able to deal with them, far better than we can. And he will deal with them, if we let them go and put them in his hands. "Cast your cares on the LORD and he will sustain you; he will never let the righteous fall" (Ps 55:22 NIV)." "Thou dost keep him in perfect peace, whose mind is stayed on thee, because he trusts in thee" (Isa 26:3). "The LORD is good, a stronghold in the day of trouble; he knows those who take refuge in him" (Nah 1:7). These are only a few of the verses that we can stand on when we need peace.

The Gethsemane narrative ends with a puzzling note about a young man wrapped in a linen cloth, who runs away naked (Mark 14:51–52; this incident is found only in the Gospel of Mark). Some scholars interpret this incident symbolically, saying that the young man is in some way connected with the young man of Mark 16:5, or represents the Christian initiate in Mark's church, awaiting baptism. But the connections are tenuous at best. Others, suggesting that the young man is a real person, have exercised their imaginations as to who he might be. Is he John son of Zebedee (though one would expect John to be with the rest of the disciples, fully clothed)? James the brother of the Lord, not yet a disciple? Mark himself, too young to be with the disciples? The angel of the Lord (but why would an angel run from humans?)? Some alternative form of Jesus himself? I suggest that without indulging in flights of fancy, we may safely say that he is a disciple, living near the garden. Wakened from sleep by the commotion of the arrest, he wraps himself in a bed sheet and rushes outside to find out what is happening. Like Peter in the next scene, he tries to follow Jesus, but is no more successful than Peter, or any of the other disciples. The Greek word for his linen cloth is *sindon*, which is also the word for a funeral shroud—the young man thinks that he is ready to die for Jesus, but he is not. Who he is we cannot say; Mark's emphasis is on the youth's failure, not his identity. The story ends on a sombre note, with Jesus under arrest and the disciples on the run. It is a good thing that the story does not end here.

WEEK 3

Jesus (and Peter) on Trial

DAY ONE

Jesus and Annas
Today's Key Verses: John 18:13, 19–24;
Mark 14:53–72; Matt. 27:3–10

THIS WEEK WE WILL study Jesus' final encounters with the Jewish authorities, plus what happened after Jesus' arrest to two disciples, Peter and Judas. Jesus' first encounter with the Jewish authorities is with Annas, the former high priest. Before we go any further, some historical information may be of interest. Annas was appointed by the Romans to the high priesthood in AD 6; in 15 he was deposed by the prefect Valerius Gratus, Pilate's predecessor. But even after this, Annas must have wielded considerable influence for decades, because five of his sons, his son-in-law Caiaphas and a grandson were all high priests. (This means that Jesus, Stephen, and James the brother of the Lord—that is, every Christian leader who was martyred in Judea before the Jewish War—all died under high priests of the house of Annas).

Please read John 18:13, 19–24. Having seized Jesus, the arresting party takes him to Annas; the scene is reported only by John. It is not a trial, but rather an interrogation, to see whether the Jewish authorities have enough of a case against Jesus to proceed further. The interrogation takes place at Annas' residence. Annas asks Jesus about His disciples (to find out whether he has political ambitions) and his teaching (to find out whether he is a heretic). It is likely that Annas already knows something about Jesus' activities. His spies have probably been in the crowds that have been listening to Jesus.

Jesus is not intimidated, even by such a formidable person as Annas. The Greek word translated "openly" in verse 20 is *parresia*. It implies speaking boldly and publicly. We may say that Jesus is doing as he instructs his disciples to do in Mark 13:11. In the Gospel of John, "the world" is a term for that which is opposed to Jesus (we will look more at this shortly). Jesus is not afraid before his opponents, because he knows that the Holy Spirit (operating in Jesus before being given to the disciples) will give him the words to say when he needs them. He provides an example for his disciples, just as he does in his prayer in Gethsemane. He says what God wants him to say, without fear or favor.

In the culture of first-century Israel, for a man of little social status, such as Jesus, to be so bold to a man of high social status, such as Annas, is an insult to Annas's honor. Such impertinence cannot be ignored. That is why in John 18:22 a temple attendant slaps Jesus across the face and scolds him for answering the high priest in such an impudent way. But a slap across the face is also an insult. But Jesus refuses to be intimidated. If he has spoken wrongly, they can testify to the wrong (i.e., they can charge him with contempt of court). But what he has told them is true, so they have no right to strike him.

1. On what other occasions has Jesus spoken boldly?

Not that this is the first time that Jesus has spoken boldly. In Mark 7:1–23 he criticizes the Pharisees for valuing "the tradition of the elders" (verses 3, 5) more highly than the commandment of God. He then says that what makes a person unclean is not eating the wrong foods, but having wrong attitudes. To Jews of that day, both statements would be startlingly radical. Only a man who was not afraid of the Pharisees would say things like this. In Matt 11:20–24 Jesus reproaches the cities of Choraizin, Bethsaida, and Capernaum, because they have not repented even though they have seen his miracles. And the running debate between Jesus and "the Jews" (i.e., the Jewish authorities) in the Gospel of John is an important feature of that Gospel (see John 5:19–47; 8:12–59; 10:22–39). But the boldest indictment of the Pharisees by Jesus must surely be the "woes" of Matt 23:1–36, where he blasts them for hypocrisy and greeed. Obviously, Jesus was not afraid to be bold when boldness was called for!

Disciples of Jesus must be prepared to be bold when necessary, just as he was. The early disciples learned to imitate Jesus in this way, though not until after Pentecost (see Acts 2:14–40; 3:12–26; 4:8–13; 5:29–32; 7:2–53). So also today, disciples of Jesus must be ready to speak out boldly for him when it is necessary. We need not worry ahead of time about what to say in such a situation, because the Holy Spirit will give us the words to say, when we need to say them (Mark 13:11). Our part is to trust him and not to be ashamed to be identified as disciples of Jesus.

2. Have you been in a situation where you were called on to speak boldly for Jesus? If it is appropriate, why not share with the group?

It is interesting that Jesus says that he has spoken openly to the *world*. The Greek word for "world" is *kosmos*, and it is an important word in the Gospel of John. Jesus' opponents are of this world, while Jesus is not (John 8:23). That is why they hate him (John 15:18), and will rejoice at his apparent destruction. But God loves the world (John 3:16), and has sent his only Son, so that through the Son the world might be saved and not condemned (John 3:17). That is why Jesus declares to the world what he has heard from God (8:26). Jesus' disciples are, like him, not of this world, because he has called them out of the world. Therefore they can expect to be hated and persecuted by the world, just as Jesus has been (John 16:33). Jesus sends them into the world as his agents, just as the Father sent him (John 17:18; 20:21). They are to continue his mission in the world of preaching, teaching, and calling out of the world those who believe.

It is interesting that Jesus says that he has always spoken in synagogues and in the temple. He preached to Jews, within the context of Jewish faith. While the disciples were eventually to preach "to the ends of the earth" (Acts 1:8), Jesus himself came to reach "the lost sheep of the house of Israel" (Matt 15:24). He did not turn away Gentiles who came looking for him (see, e.g., Matt 8:5–13; 15:21–28). But his main focus was on reaching his own people, before sending the message of salvation further abroad (compare "to the Jew first, and also to the Greek," Rom 1:16). His desire was for—dare I say it?—revival among the Jewish people. Since "revival" is a "Christianese" word that gets a lot of use in some parts of the church, I should clarify what I mean. In his preaching, Jesus called the Jewish people back to a right relationship with God. To the kind of relationship which God wanted to have with them right from the beginning. This, I suggest, is the meaning of the Sermon on the Mount (Matt 5–7). We cannot study the Sermon on the Mount here; let me just say that in the Sermon Jesus is calling the people to move beyond the letter of the law to living by the intention of the law. Living by the intention of the law is how the people's righteousness can exceed the righteousness of the scribes and Pharisees (Matt 5:20), and how they can live the way God wants them to. For example, the law forbids murder, but Jesus condemns anger, which can lead to murder. And the law forbids adultery, but Jesus warns against lust, which is the first step toward adultery.

Jesus' preaching is thus in line with the preaching of the Old Testament prophets, who also call Israel back to a right relationship with God. In Isa 1:15–17, for example, God says, "Even though you make many prayers, I will not listen; your hands are full of blood. Wash yourselves; make yourselves clean; remove the evil of your doings from before my eyes; cease to do evil; learn to do good; seek justice, correct oppression; defend the fatherless, plead for the widow." And in Isa 29:13 (quoted by Jesus in Mark 7:6–7) God says, "this people draw near to me with their lips, but their heart is far from me, and their fear of me is a commandment of men learned by rote." And Hos 6:6 (quoted by Jesus in Matt 9:13), says, "I desire steadfast love and not sacrifice, the knowledge of God, rather than burnt offerings." Jeremiah receives a message from God: "Add your burnt offerings to your sacrifices, and eat the flesh. For in the day that I brought them out of the land of Egypt, I did not speak to your fathers or command them concerning burnt offerings and sacrifices. But this command I gave them, 'Obey my voice, and I will be your God, and you shall be my people; and walk in all the way that I command you, that it may be well with you.' But they did not obey or incline their ear, but walked in their own counsels and the stubbornness of their evil hearts, and went backward and not forward" (Jer 7:21–24). And again, "How can you say, 'We are wise, and the law of the LORD is with us'? But behold, the false pen of the scribes has made it into a lie" (Jer 8:8). We can see, then, that Jesus not only fulfills prophecy; he carries on its traditions in his own preaching.

We may also note that Jesus answers Annas only with respect to his teaching. To protect his disciples, he will say nothing about them. About his teaching he says that he has always taught openly and never said anything in secret. Therefore, he implies, Annas will have no trouble detecting whether he is a heretic or not, without asking him any questions. A heretic would be likely to teach his heresy in secret, to avoid getting caught. This Jesus has not done. He calls on Annas to ask those who heard him what he said. He is in effect asking for a trial. So Annas obliges him by sending him to Caiaphas, the ruling high priest.

DAY TWO

Jesus and the Sanhedrin
Today's Key Verses: Mark 14:53–59

Yesterday we looked at the first stage of Jesus' encounter with the Jewish authorities, his interrogation by Annas. Today we will begin looking at the second stage, his appearance before the rulers of Israel. Annas has decided that there is enough evidence against Jesus to proceed further, so Jesus is taken to the council. Please read Mark 14:53–59, the first part of Mark's report of Jesus' appearance before the Sanhedrin, the ruling council of the Jews. The Sanhedrin consisted of seventy-one of Israel's leading priests, including the high priest, who presided over it. Mark does not name Caiaphas, but Matthew and John name him in their accounts of Jesus' appearance before the Sanhedrin, and Luke names him in Luke 3:2. Again, a little historical information may be of interest before we go further. Joseph Caiaphas was high priest from AD 18 to 37. Since during the Roman occupation the average term of a high priest was four years, his nineteen-year term is remarkable, and shows his political skill. He was appointed by Gratus and deposed by Pilate's successor, Vitellius.

Jesus' encounter with Caiaphas takes place at Caiaphas's residence rather than the courthouse, which suggests that the proceedings are not formal. Many have complained about alleged breaches of procedure by the Sanhedrin. Two things must be said about this. First, those who talk about breaches of procedure usually cite Jewish writings from 150 to 200 years after Jesus' death, and it is not certain that the rules found in these writings were in force in the first century. We may also note that none of the Gospel writers says anything about the actions of the Jewish authorities being illegal (unlike in Acts 23:3, where Paul protests that the way the Jewish authorities are treating him is "contrary to the law"). Second, there is nothing in the Gospel accounts that suggests that Jesus' encounter with the Sanhedrin is not an informal investigation, or a preliminary hearing, rather than a formal trial. The Sanhedrin wants to find out if it has enough of a case against Jesus for them to take the case to Pilate. Seeing the matter in this way lessens the difficulties considerably.

Some claim that there was no way for the church to find out what really happened at Jesus' trials. But Peter, in the high priest's courtyard, may have been able to learn something. And John mentions another disciple, known to the high priest, who was there (John 18:15). Besides, many leading Jews came to believe in Jesus (John 12:42)—Nicodemus and Joseph of Arimathea are mentioned by name. All these could have provided information.

Let us turn to Mark's narrative. The scene takes place at night, ending at dawn or shortly after. Mark, a skilful storyteller, switches from Jesus (verse 53) to Peter (verse 54), back to Jesus (verses 55–65), back to Peter again (verses 66–72), and ends with Jesus (Mark 15:1). This is how Mark shows that the questioning of Jesus by the Sanhedrin and the questioning of Peter by those in the courtyard take place at the same time. But we notice that Mark begins and ends with Jesus, keeping him the overall main focus. The word "against" sounds through the story like a funeral bell. Verses 55 and 56 refer to false testimony *against* Jesus, and in verse 60 the high priest asks Jesus, "What is it that these men testify *against* you?" The Greek word translated "condemned" in verse 64 literally means "passed sentence *against*." Mark puts "against" at the beginning, middle, and end of his account, emphasizing the hostility that Jesus faces.

The arresting party takes Jesus to the high priest. In Mark 14:53 Mark says that they take him to the high priest, not that they take him to the courthouse. This may mean that they take him to the high priest's residence. This is confirmed by verse 54 and by John 18:28, "Then they led him from the house of Caiaphas to the praetorium." That Jesus' encounter with the Sanhedrin takes place at Caiaphas' residence is an indication that it is a preliminary hearing, not a trial.

The Sanhedrin find witnesses willing to testify against Jesus, but their statements are invalid because they do not agree. The testimony is inconsistent because it is false. False testimony (what we call perjury) violates the ninth commandment (Exod 20:16). That is why Jewish law required the consistent testimony of two or more witnesses for a conviction (Deut 17:6; 19:15). Finally two men say that they heard Jesus make a statement about the temple (a garbled version of John 2:19), but there is still an inconsistency (presumably as to the details of exactly when and where Jesus supposedly made this statement). In John 2:19 Jesus says, "Destroy this temple, and in three days I will raise it up." The witnesses of Mark 14:58 claim that he said, "I will destroy this temple." But what he actually says means that his opponents will destroy the temple. "The Jews," to whom he is speaking, take his words literally, and assume that he is referring to the temple building. An understandable misunderstanding, since they are standing in the temple courts. But he is speaking symbolically, not literally, referring to his death and resurrection. John, writing after the fact, understands this. But he makes it clear that even Jesus' disciples did not understand at the time what he meant (John 2:21–22).

3. Have you ever had someone say that you did something that you did not do? If it is appropriate, why not share with the group?

Having someone say something false about you, even if it is not an accusation to the police, is very painful. If you are in this situation, Jesus knows what you are going through. He understands how difficult it is for you, because he has been there. And he is able to help you. God is a God of truth, and Jesus himself is the Truth (John 14:6). He knows the truth of your situation. He is able to bring the truth out so that others know it too. Trust God to intervene on your behalf. He knows what is happening, and he will deal with it if you put it in his hands.

David also knew what it is like to be falsely accused. This is another connection between him and Jesus. Saul in his jealousy thinks that David is planning to harm him (1 Sam. 22:13; 24:9). But David has no such intention, and refuses to harm Saul when he has the opportunity (1 Sam 24:1–7; 26:6–12). David expresses his feelings about the situation in several of his Psalms. He is distressed by the circumstances, but still feels absolutely confident that God will bring the truth out (Pss 7; 12; 17; 35).

4. How is Jesus' behavior before the Sanhedrin an example to us?

1 Pet 2:21–23 NRSV says, "For to this you have been called, because Christ also suffered for you, leaving you an example, that you should follow in his steps. 'He committed no sin, and no guile was found in his mouth.' When he was abused, he did not return abuse; when he suffered, he did not threaten; but he entrusted himself to the one who

judges justly." During all this mistreatment, Jesus did not return insult for insult, or lash out in any way. Instead, he entrusted himself to God, who judges justly. (Interestingly, the word that Peter uses for "entrusted" is *paradidomi*, the same word that the Gospel writers use repeatedly for Jesus being "handed over" or "betrayed." At the same time, and in the same way, as Jesus is handed over to the authorities, he hands himself over to God). In this way he provides an example for us to follow when we are mistreated. In this kind of situation, it is tempting to take things into our own hands. That is what the flesh wants. But the best thing we can do is to trust our situation to God. He is a God of justice, and if we trust him, he will be our Vindicator. He is also our Deliverer, and he is able to turn even the worst of situations around, for our good and his glory. But we must be careful to put things entirely into God's hands, and take our hands off. God will not take matters into his hands while we keep them in our hands. In fact, our "dealing with" a situation can block God from dealing with it. We must trust him and wait for him to intervene. He may not act when we want him to, or in the way we want him to. But if we trust him, he will act, in his way and in his time.

David also knew what it is like to be attacked by enemies. He also knew how to trust God for vindication. "The LORD is my light and my salvation; whom shall I fear? When evildoers assail me, uttering slanders against me . . . they shall stumble and fall. Though a host encamp against me, my heart shall not fear; though war arise against me, yet I will be confident" (Ps 27:1–3). "Commit your way to the LORD; trust in him, and he will act. He will bring forth your vindication as the light, and your right as the noonday" (Ps. 37:5–6). "But I call upon God; and the LORD will save me. Evening and morning and at noon I utter my complaint and moan, and he will hear my voice. He will deliver my soul from the battle that I wage, for many are arrayed against me" (Ps 55:16–18). And David does not forget to respond when God does deliver him; Psalm 18 is a thanksgiving for deliverance.

DAY THREE

A Sheep Before Its Shearers
Today's Key Verses: Mark 14:60–65

Yesterday we looked at the first part of Jesus' appearance before the Sanhedrin. Today we will look at the second part of this final appearance of Jesus before this Jewish high council. As we saw yesterday, the Sanhedrin try to find witnesses to testify against Jesus, but the testimony that they find is false. So Caiaphas takes charge. He tries to push Jesus into replying to the false testimony, but Jesus refuses to dignify it with an answer. In another sense, one may see Scripture being fulfilled in his silence (compare Isa. 53:7, "He was oppressed, and he was afflicted, yet he opened not his mouth; like a lamb that is led to the slaughter, and like a sheep that before its shearers is dumb, so he opened not his mouth"). It is another matter, however, when Caiaphas asks him flatly if he is the Messiah and Son of God.

5. Until this point in the Gospel, Jesus has been secretive about his identity as Messiah. Why does he answer Caiaphas here?

The time for silence and the possibility of misunderstanding are both past. Who is likely to believe that Jesus, abandoned, arrested, under threat of a death sentence, is a glorious military Messiah? There can be no doubt now about what kind of Messiah Jesus is. He comes to his glory through suffering.

We should look briefly at Jesus' answer to Caiaphas at verse 62. Caiaphas asks Jesus if he is the Messiah and son of the Blessed (i.e., God). But when Jesus answers, he does not use either of those terms. Rather he describes himself as the Son of man. What does this term "Son of man" mean? It is awkward in Greek, and in English (something we can miss because we are so familiar with it), but not in Hebrew. "Son of man" translates the Hebrew *ben adam*, which is the standard expression for a human being. In the Old Testament, God calls Ezekiel *ben adam* more than ninety times (Ezek. 2:1, 6, 8; 3:1, 4, 10, 17, 25, etc.; KJV, NIV, and RSV translate "son of man," while other English versions have "man," "mortal," "mortal man," or "son of dust." The last one takes account of the fact that in Hebrew *adam* means "dust" as well as "man;" compare Gen

2:7). In this way God emphasizes the contrast between the holy Giver of the messages and the human prophet who receives them, representing his race. God is a holy God, Ezekiel is a sinful human. But there is also the "one like a son of man" of Dan 7:13, a figure who looks like a man, but is given supernatural power and glory.

In the New Testament, "Son of man" is the only expression that Jesus uses to describe himself, and, oddly, no one else uses it about him (it is equally odd that the same trend is seen in our hymns and worship. Songwriters use a number of titles for Jesus, but rarely use the title that Jesus used of himself). But what does Jesus mean when he calls himself the Son of man? The phrase is associated with his suffering, because he uses it as he foretells his death. But every time he predicts his death, he also predicts his resurrection. And the Son of man is Lord of the Sabbath. In Jesus the Son of man, both of the Old Testament meanings of the phrase are combined. In one sense, he is the representative Man, humanity as it should have been. This is why he can give his life as a ransom for many (Mark 10:45), and it is what Paul means when he calls Jesus the last Adam (Rom 5:12-19; 1 Cor 15:45-49). But Jesus the Son of man will also come in judgment and glory (Mark 8:38; 13:26-27; Matt 11:27; 24:27, 30-31; John 5:22-24, 27-29). It is only here, in the Passion, that the two ideas come together, because Jesus' glory and power are fully revealed only in his suffering on our behalf. How unexpected God's ways are, and how different from ours!

Jesus says that his opponents will see him seated at the right hand of Power (i.e. of God). The right hand is the position of honor, so this is a way of saying that one day his opponents will see him vindicated by God. His coming in the clouds reminds the reader of Dan. 7:13. It refers to his second coming at the end of history. Again we see him vindicated as God gives him glory. This event is something that every human will see. Those who happen to be alive when it happens will see it from earth. The dead who turned to Jesus for salvation and received forgiveness for their sins before they died will see it from heaven. Those who died in their sins will see it from hell. We do not know when this will happen, and should not spend too much energy trying to figure out when it will happen (Acts 1:7). Our part is to make sure that we are ready, by maintaining a close relationship with God, and to warn others to be ready.

When Jesus says this, that is enough for Caiaphas. Jesus' statement insults God's honor and glory, and that brings it within the definition of blasphemy used in the first century (later the definition was narrowed). So Caiaphas rips his garments as a sign of distress at hearing blasphemy (compare 2 Kings 18:37; 19:1). This is another indication that this encounter is not a formal trial. The high priest was not permitted to tear his robes (Lev 10:6; 21:10), so Caiaphas must not be wearing them here. It is interesting that blasphemy is the first charge that Jesus' opponents make against him, if only to themselves (Mark 2:7). Here it is also the last charge that they make against him.

Having decided that Jesus has spoken blasphemy and thus deserves to die, some of the Sanhedrin show their disapproval of his blasphemy by spitting on him and playing a rough version of the game that we know today as blind man's buff. They blindfold him and call on him to know by the Messiah's prophetic insight which one of them hits him. Jesus has predicted that he would be rejected and mistreated by the authorities (Mark 8:31; 9:31; 10:33–34). The Sanhedrists are demanding that Jesus prove that he is the Messiah by a sign, as they have done before (e.g., Matt 12:38; 16:1; Mark 8:11; Luke 11:16). The irony is that Jesus has given them many signs, in the form of his preaching, teaching, and deeds of power. But they have not been able to recognize them.

6. What wrong attitudes do the Jewish authorities have, and how can we avoid them?

Perhaps the most obvious of their wrong attitudes is that they "put God in a box." By Jesus' time, Israel had a long history of dealings with God. Not surprising, then, that they should come to some conclusions about what God is like. The problem was that over time, these conclusions hardened into preconceptions. The religious leaders of the Jews had come to believe that they knew all about what God is like and how he should act, and no one was going to tell them any different. So when God did something new in Jesus, they were not prepared for it and could not accept it, because what God did in Jesus was not what they were expecting him to do.

We must not fool ourselves into thinking that we are immune to this same attitude. To think otherwise is dangerous pride, and opens the door for us to fall into their sin. We must remember that the Jews genuinely loved God and wanted to please him. That is why they developed the oral and written traditions which they called "a fence around the law." They wanted to know exactly how God wanted them to live under the law. For example, the law commanded them to do no work on the Sabbath. But which activities were considered "work," and which were not? What if someone got sick and needed a doctor? What should a farmer do if one of his animals fell into a well on the Sabbath—was he allowed to pull it out? Could a woman prepare meals on the Sabbath? The oral and written traditions clarified how to apply the law to everyday situations.

Some two thousand years after Jesus' death, the church of the twenty-first century, like Israel of the first century, has a long history of dealings with God. She has developed many rich traditions which many of her people love. These traditions have their value. But we must never confuse traditions with the doctrines found in the written Word of God. I am not calling for change for change's sake, or the wholesale dismissal of what comes from the church's past. But we should be able to set aside traditions that contradict the Word, or that interfere in any way with our service to God. A church that cannot do so is in danger of losing its vitality. It has rightly been said that the seven last words of the church are, "We've never done it that way before." This is the problem that Jesus is talking about in his analogy of the wine and the wineskins (Luke 5:37–39). New wine, he says, cannot be put into old wineskins. It will burst them, so it must be put into new ones. Ironically, people who have drunk old wine usually think that it is better than the new.

The Jewish authorities' second wrong attitude is connected to the first. Not only have they become set in their attitudes about God, they are unwilling to listen when someone tells them something that does not fit in with their ideas. In other words, they are not teachable. They think that they know better than anyone else. The root of this problem is, plainly and simply, pride. As we saw last week, pride is an attitude that has plagued humans since the beginning, and we dare not think that we are immune to it. We must be humble enough to keep from thinking that we know it all and have nothing left to learn from anyone else.

Finally, we may say that the Jewish authorities, in their eagerness to please God under the law, had come to focus on rules rather than relationship in their dealings with him. This is why they are so displeased when Jesus does things which, in their view, break the Sabbath laws (see, e.g., Mark 2:23–28; 3:1–6; Luke 14:1–6; John 5:1–18; 9:1–34). This trap of legalism is one that we also can easily fall into. As humans, it is easier for us to think that we can satisfy God by certain actions than to get involved in the more complicated and less clear-cut task of having a relationship with him. This is why, on one occasion, the crowd asks Jesus what work God wants them to do. Jesus answers that what God wants them to do is to believe in himself, the one whom God has sent (John 6:28-29). It has often been said that the Christian life is not about rules, it is about relationship. But there is something that must be said here. Too often we evangelical Christians accuse other denominations within the church of being legalistic. But we also are being legalistic when we say, "How can she come to church dressed like that?" or, "How can he go out drinking on Saturday night and come to church on Sunday morning?" or, "You are not a good Christian if you do not pray for X minutes a day/ read your Bible for X minutes a day/ come to every meeting at the church." We must avoid at all costs these attitudes toward our brothers and sisters in Christ. We must avoid judging others (Matt 7:1), because we usually do not know all the facts about other people or their circumstances. We can only see a person's outward appearance; only God can look into a human heart (1 Sam 16:7). Our brothers and sisters in Christ are accountable to God, not to us (Rom 14:4). If they are sinning, God will convict them of their sin and help them turn away from it, when he is ready and they are ready.

DAY FOUR

A Black Sheep in the Courtyard
Today's Key Verses: Mark 14:66-72

So far this week we have studied Jesus' appearances before the Jewish authorities. We saw that he is neither intimidated nor defensive. Like his ancestor David, he entrusts his situation entirely to God. Today and tomorrow we will focus on two of his disciples. Even as Jesus is being questioned, one of his disciples is also being questioned—and is not doing very well. Please read Mark 14:66-72. Peter has followed Jesus "at a distance," but a disciple who wants to be under Jesus' protection must stay close to him. John says in one of his letters, "We know that those who are born of God do not sin, but the one who was born of God [i.e., Jesus] protects them, and the evil one does not touch them" (1 John 5:18). And in John 11:9-10 Jesus says, "If any one walks in the day, he does not stumble, because he sees the light of this world. But if anyone walks in the night, he stumbles, because the light is not in him." Since he has already said that he is the Light of the World (John 8:12; 9:5), he is telling his disciples that they will be safe if they stay close to him.

While Jesus is unafraid before the highest Jewish authority in the land, Peter caves in at the first pressure, and that from a servant girl. In Mark 3:14, 16 Jesus calls Peter to be with him. But in Mark 14:67–68, when the maid says that Peter was with Jesus, he denies it. In other words, he denies that he is a disciple.

Peter moves away, but not far enough to be safe. The others in the courtyard can tell that Peter is a Galilean, presumably by his accent (compare Matt 26:73), so they assume that Peter is a disciple of Jesus the Galilean. It is not long before he has said three times that he is not a disciple of Jesus. He calls down curses on himself (this does not involve the ancient Israeli equivalent of four-letter words, but something like "May God strike me dead if I am lying"), and takes an oath that he is not a disciple of Jesus (was being denied by a friend as painful to Jesus as his physical mistreatment by enemies?). Even as the Sanhedrin mock Jesus' prophetic ability, his most recent prophecy (compare Mark 14:30) is being fulfilled. When the rooster crows, Peter remembers what Jesus said, and breaks down and weeps. Here again we see Jesus as the Prophet whose prophecy is trustworthy because it is accurate. This is one of two main points in this story.

7. How does Peter set himself up for failure?

The other main point in this story, besides the accuracy of Jesus' prophecy, is Peter's failure. Peter's biggest mistake is assuming that he knows better than Jesus. When Jesus tells Peter that he will deny him (Mark 14:30), Peter replies, in effect, "No way!" But when what Jesus predicted happens, Peter remembers what Jesus said (Mark 14:72). In Gethsemane, Jesus warns the disciples to stay alert and pray, or they will be in danger. But Peter, like the other disciples, does not take Jesus' advice. Instead of praying, he goes to sleep, which leaves him off-guard at the crucial moment. When the pressure comes, Peter is unprepared, so he caves in. The root problem here is that he puts too much confidence in himself. He does not yet understand that he cannot follow Jesus under his own power. His courage is based on pride and self-reliance rather than on humble reliance on God. This leads him to talk and act without thinking, to talk when he should be listening, and to be with the wrong companions at the fire when he should stay away. By the time the night is over, Peter's pride is broken, and he has learned that "Pride goes before destruction, and a haughty spirit before a fall" (Prov. 16:18), and humility is the only thing that will prevent such a disaster.

Peter's second mistake is that he seeks approval from humans rather than God. In other words, he is intimidated by the people in the courtyard when they question him. But Jesus has told his disciples earlier whom they should fear. "And do not fear those who can kill the body but cannot kill the soul; rather fear him who can destroy both soul and body in hell" (Matt. 10:28). Peter does not yet realize that one who is more in awe of God than of anyone else need not be afraid of anyone at all, because God will protect his own. "This I know, that God is for me . . . in God I trust without a fear. What can man do to me?" says the Psalmist (Ps 56:9, 11).

We must remember that if it can happen to Peter, it can happen to us. We must guard against his mistakes of overconfidence and fear of people rather than God. We must have the humility to realize that we cannot follow Jesus under our own power; we must have the help and protection of the Holy Spirit. If we do not, we make ourselves vulnerable and will fail as surely as Peter did. We must also not allow ourselves to be intimidated by other people. We should trust in God's protection and favor as we do what he wants us to do.

There are a few more things to say briefly before we leave this passage. If Peter denies Jesus by what he says, the other disciples deny him by being absent. If Peter denies Jesus here, he does better when he himself is before the Sanhedrin (Acts 4:5–20). Peter's courage fails temporarily, but his faith does not. Jesus has prayed that Peter's faith would not fail, and that when Peter has recovered from his stumble, he would strengthen the other disciples (Luke 22:32). We see the first part of this prophecy fulfilled here; we will see later what happens concerning the second part. Finally, if Peter had denied himself, as disciples are called to do, he would not have denied Jesus. But we must also say that, as we will see later, God brought good out of Peter's stumble. For now we will only note that if Peter had not denied Jesus, he probably would have died that night, which was not God's plan for him.

8. Please read John 10:1-15. What connections can you see between the characters in this passage and the characters in this first part of the Passion narrative?

In John 10, Jesus describes himself as the Good Shepherd who gives his life for the sheep. Here in the Passion narrative, we see Jesus acting like the Good Shepherd. In the midst of his struggle in Gethsemane, he is concerned for his disciples' welfare, and he will give his life for them. But there is more. In John 10:10 Jesus mentions the thief; we saw last week that Judas is a thief. And in John 10:12-13, Jesus mentions the hireling. The hired hand, Jesus says, has no commitment to the sheep, because they do not belong to him. He is only concerned with getting paid. So when the wolf attacks the flock, he runs away. This reminds the reader of how Peter acts in the Passion narrative (but in Week 7 we will see that this is not the end of the story). Connected with this is a "pun" which is apparent in Greek but not in English. The Greek word for "courtyard" is *aule*, which is also the word for "sheepfold." Peter in the high priest's courtyard acts like the hired hand in the sheepfold. This is an example of how intricately John, as inspired storyteller, weaves his story.

DAY FIVE

The Field of Blood
Today's Key Verses: Matt 27:3-10

Yesterday we looked at what happened to Peter after Jesus' arrest, and saw Jesus' chief disciple get a painful lesson in humility. Today we will look at what happened to Judas; please read Matt 27:3-10. Matthew places his story of the disciple who denied Jesus (Matt 26:69-75) beside the story of the disciple who betrayed him. Thus Matthew invites the reader to compare Judas's reaction to failure with Peter's. As one scholar puts it, "Whereas Peter's remorse leads to repentance, Judas's leads to terminal despair."[1]

9. What differences do you see between Peter and Judas?

We can see three significant differences between Peter and Judas. First, when Satan attacks, Peter pulls himself together and rallies, but Judas

---

1. Keener, *Matthew*, 656.

gives in. Second, Peter's faith fails only temporarily, while Judas' faith fails permanently. This is why Peter is able to rally while Judas gives in. Third, Peter still loves Jesus, but Judas loves money more than Jesus. Jesus has said earlier that no one can serve God and money at the same time. They will end up loving one and hating the other (Matt 6:24). There is also a significant difference in how Matthew ends his stories of Peter and Judas. Peter "went out and wept bitterly" (Matt 26:75), but Judas "went and hanged himself" (Matt 27:5). This is the last thing that Matthew says about each of these men. But we must say that Jesus did not love Judas any less than he loved Peter.

Judas reacts when he sees that Jesus has been convicted. It is as if he has not expected things to go so far. Perhaps he has not thought things through, and has underestimated how badly the Jewish authorities want to destroy Jesus. Perhaps he has not wanted things to go so far, if he intended to pressure Jesus into making a move that would show him as Messiah.

In Matt. 27:3, the RSV says that Judas "repented." But the NIV is more correct when it says that he "was seized with remorse." The Greek word used here is not the usual word for repenting, which is *metanoeo*. The Greek word used in Matt 27:3 is *metamellomai*: its most usual meaning is "to feel regret; change one's mind." Judas feels regret and remorse for what he has done, but he does not repent.

So then, what is the difference between remorse and true biblical repentance, which leads to forgiveness? Remorse simply feels regret for sin. Repentance feels regret for sin, but it does not stop there. David knew the joy of being forgiven. "Blessed is he whose transgression is forgiven, whose sin is covered" (Ps 32:1). He felt the discomfort of conviction until he dealt with his sin: "When I declared not my sin, my body wasted away through my groaning all day long . . . I acknowledged my sin to thee, and I did not hide my iniquity. I said, 'I will confess my transgressions to the LORD'; then thou didst forgive the guilt of my sin" Ps 32:3, 5). True repentance is humble. It acknowledges sin as sin—no excuses—and that it needs God's help and forgiveness. And it does not hide from God, it runs to him. The last part of Ps 32:5 is important. Having confessed his sin and asked God for forgiveness, David accepts God's forgiveness and knows that he is forgiven. Sometimes this is difficult, especially if we have the idea that we do not deserve to be forgiven. The truth is that none of us deserves to be forgiven. But—thank God!—God does not forgive us on the basis of whether we deserve it or not. He forgives us because he is a loving, forgiving, merciful God. He does not forgive us because of who we are, but because of who he is.

Paul also has something to say about repentance. He had written a scolding letter to the church at Corinth. Confronting the issues had caused him, and them, a lot of pain. But they had responded well, and Paul is able to commend them. "For even if I made you sorry with my letter, I do not regret it (though I did regret it), for I see that that letter grieved you, if only for a little while. As it is, I rejoice, not because you were grieved, but because you were grieved into repenting; for you felt a godly grief, so that you suffered no loss through us. For godly grief produces a repentance that leads to salvation and brings no regret, but worldly grief produces death. For see what earnestness this godly grief has produced in you, what eagerness to clear yourselves, what indignation, what alarm, what longing, what zeal, what punishment! At every point you have proved yourselves guiltless in the matter" (2 Cor 7:8–11).

Someone who truly repents, then, starts by seeing their sin the way God sees it, as sin. They acknowledge their need of forgiveness, and go to God for forgiveness and cleansing. They accept his forgiveness and move on into changed behavior, leaving the sin behind. This is how we are freed from sin, so that Satan cannot use past sin to drag us down.

Judas tries to make up for what he has done by returning the money that he took to betray Jesus. But the Jewish authorities refuse to take it back. They say, in effect, "Your guilt is not our problem." No human action can atone for sin; we can only have forgiveness for sins because of what Jesus did on Calvary. This means that Judas is going to the wrong place for forgiveness. He needs to go to Jesus rather than the chief priests.

Judas confesses that he has "betrayed innocent blood." It seems to bother him more that he has betrayed someone innocent than that he has betrayed the Master with whom he has lived and worked for so long. The shedding of innocent blood is an important theme in the Gospel of Matthew. At Matt 23:30, for example, Jesus says that the Pharisees claim that they would not have shed the blood of the prophets as their ancestors did. But in fact "all the righteous blood shed on earth" (Matt 23:35) will fall on them. Not least, there is the blood of the innocent, sinless Jesus, "poured out for many for the forgiveness of sins" (Matt 26:28).

Since Judas is unable to make things right through the Jewish authorities, he gives in to despair, and goes out and hangs himself. He thinks that he is beyond God's forgiveness. But in fact, this is arrogance because it means that he thinks that his sin is too big for God to handle. He is as arrogant as Peter, though in a different way. His end helps to make another connection between Jesus and David. Because the only other person in the Bible to hang himself is David's advisor Ahithophel, who went over to David's son Absalom when Absalom rebelled (2 Sam 17:23).

Another thing that may be said about Judas is that his sin progresses. His greed leads to him first to steal from the common fund, thus abusing the trust given to him as treasurer (John 12:6). This opens the door for Satan to work in his life (John 13:2, 27). Soon he accepts more money to betray Jesus. Finally his despair leads to self-destruction.

10. What lessons for ourselves can we learn from the story of Judas?

One thing that we can learn from the story of Judas concerns sin. As I just said, Judas's sin progresses. What if he had recognized his greed for what it was and gone to Jesus for forgiveness? It is important that we be alert for sin in our lives, and deal with it as soon as we see it. A wise gardener pulls the weeds out before they grow big. Or as Martin Luther put it, "You cannot keep the birds from flying over your head, but you can keep them from making a nest in your hair." The Holy Spirit will help us to detect sin in our lives. As soon as he shows it to us, we must run to Jesus for forgiveness and cleansing.

Second, Judas thinks that he is beyond God's forgiveness. That is also a lie from Satan, and we must not buy into it. No one is beyond God's forgiveness, and there is nothing that God will not forgive if we truly repent. To think otherwise is arrogant pride. There is no sin that we can dream up, let alone actually commit, that God will refuse to forgive if we come to him in humble repentance and ask him to forgive us. "The steadfast love of the LORD never ceases, his mercies never come to an end; they are new every morning; great is your faithfulness" (Lam 3:22–23). I have had callers to the Prayer Line in the middle of the night say that they have sinned, and God will not forgive them, because his day's supply of mercy has run out. They seem to imagine him getting a delivery of mercy from somewhere every morning, or making a fresh batch of mercy for himself every morning! But that makes verse 23 contradict verse 22, which says that God never runs out of mercy. "For you, O LORD, are good and forgiving, abounding in steadfast love to all who call on you," says David (Ps 86:5).

Third, we can learn something from this story about the danger of despair. Despair is the opposite of hope, it says that there is no hope. God is the God of hope (Rom 15:13), but despair gives up on God. This is why some parts of the church have listed despair as one of the seven deadly sins. Despair says that the circumstances are too difficult for God to deal with. But nothing is too difficult for him (Jer 32:17). So there is a sense in which despair is the opposite of faith and trust, because faith and trust do not give up on God. In a bad situation, we must choose to trust that God will bring us through. If we give in to despair, it will destroy us (Prov 15:13). Do not give up on God! That is not always easy. But if you keep your eyes on God instead of your circumstances, he will not abandon you or let you down.

The Jewish authorities decide that they cannot put the money back into the Temple treasury; this indicates that they are aware of their wrongdoing. Indeed bribery was considered even more blameworthy in ancient Mediterranean society than it is in our own. So they use the money to buy a potter's field, to use as a burial ground for foreigners who die in Jerusalem. In another sense, the reader also sees Scripture being fulfilled. When Matthew says that the Scriptures are being fulfilled, he is implying that God knew in advance about the things that are happening. This is a point that Matthew makes more than once in his Passion narrative (Matt 26:54, 56; 27:9). And there are other places where he makes a literary reference to the Scriptures which a reader familiar with the Scriptures would recognize (Matt 26:64/Dan 7:13, Ps 110:1; Matt 27:24/Deut 21:6–9, Ps 26:6; Matt 27:35/Ps 22:18; Matt 27:39/Ps 22:7–8, Ps 109:25; Matt 27:46/Ps 22:1; Matt 27:33/Ps 69:21). In this way Matthew says that God is in control. As chaotic as things may seem to be to the disciples, they are not beyond God's control. The same is true in our lives. God watches over us with a Father's love and care. Even when our circumstances are beyond our control, they are not beyond God's control. He is in charge, and he knows what he is doing, even when we do not know what he is doing. Just as he brought good out of Jesus' suffering, he will bring good out of ours.

The Scripture which Matthew quotes is in fact not from Jeremiah, but is Zech 11:13. But Matthew has not made a mistake. He wants the reader to think also of Jeremiah's potter, breaking and remaking Israel as he sees fit (Jer 18:1–11), and the field of Jer 32:6–15, purchased by Jeremiah as a sign of the hope of restoration. Because the people of God are being redefined. They are no longer the physical descendants of Abraham, Isaac and Jacob, but those who believe in Jesus. And in the suffering and death of Jesus lies the only hope of humanity's restoration from its fallen state. It is only by his sacrifice that the world's sin is taken away (John 1:29, 36), and the world is redeemed. "[Christ] gave himself for us to redeem us from all iniquity and to purify for himself a people of his own who are zealous for good works" (Titus 2:14; compare 1 Pet 1:18–19; Rev 5:9).

WEEK 4

A Roman Tragedy

DAY ONE

Pilate Meets Jesus
Today's key verses: *John 18:28–19:26; Luke 23:6–12; Matt 27:19, 24–25*

THIS WEEK WE WILL study Jesus' trial before the Roman authorities who governed Judea in the first century. If there is some question whether Jesus' appearances before the Jewish authorities should be called an interrogation, a preliminary hearing, or a trial, there is no such doubt about Jesus' appearance before Pilate. It is early morning, and the Jewish authorities have decided that Jesus has spoken blasphemy and deserves to die. So they take him to Pilate, the Roman governor, to have the sentence confirmed and carried out. Once again, a little historical information may be of interest. In fact, little is known about Pontius Pilate. It used to be said that his title was procurator. But in 1961 a stone plaque was found which reads, "Pontius Pilate, prefect of Judea." In fact it was only after AD 44 that Roman governors of Judea had the title of procurator.

Pilate served as prefect of Judea from AD 27 to 36. This nine-year term is an indication of his political skill, because only his predecessor, Valerius Gratus, served a longer term. He was a member of the class of knights, the lesser nobility. He is often said to have been cruel, but when the records are looked at objectively, he comes across as tactless and undiplomatic rather than cruel or malicious. In AD 36 there was a gathering of Samaritans at Mount Gerizim which was broken up by Pilate's soldiers; a number of people were killed. The Samaritan authorities filed a complaint with Pilate's superior, who sent him to Rome to appear before Tiberius Caesar. But by the time Pilate arrived in Rome, Tiberius had died, and Pilate disappears from history. Several other stories about him arose during the Middle Ages, but we will not concern ourselves with those here.

We will focus on John's account of the Roman trial, because it is the longest and most detailed. It is also an example of John's storytelling skill. It is like a drama with seven scenes. The structure of the passage can be set out in a chart. It looks like this:

18:28–32	outside	Pilate and "the Jews"
18:33–38a	inside	Pilate and Jesus
18:38b–40	outside	Barabbas
19:1–3	inside	Roman abuse and mockery
19:4–8	outside	Pilate and "the Jews"
19:9–11	inside	Pilate and Jesus
19:11–16	outside	Pilate and "the Jews"

When we look at the passage in this way, two things are immediately obvious. The first is that John 19:1–3, Roman abuse and mockery of Jesus, is the center part of the passage, and therefore the most important. The second is that there is an alternation between inside and outside. The Jewish leaders are outside, Jesus is inside, and Pilate shuttles back and forth between them. This physical movement is an outward expression of Pilate's state of mind, as he vacillates about what to do about Jesus. This connects to an important theme in the Gospel of John: those who encounter Jesus must choose for or against him. Pilate tries to avoid making a decision about Jesus. But because he refuses to take a stand for Jesus, he is forced to take a stand against him. Sitting on the fence is impossible. In the introduction to his film version of *Hamlet*, Laurence Olivier says, "This is the tragedy of a man who cannot make up his mind." The tragedy of Pilate is the tragedy of man who is trying to avoid having to make up his mind.

1. In 1 Kings 18:21, what does Elijah say that the people are doing? What must they do?

Elijah has told king Ahab to gather the four hundred fifty prophets of Baal whom Ahab supports and meet Elijah at Mount Carmel. It is time for a showdown. The people of Israel are also summoned, so that they can witness the encounter. The Israelites have been worshipping both God and Baal. Elijah says that they are "limping with two different opinions." Their desire to hold on to both deities is crippling them spiritually, so this state of affairs cannot go on. The people must choose whom they will serve. "If the LORD is God, follow him; but if Baal, then follow him." Israel had to make this choice right from its beginnings. "You shall have no other gods before me," (Exod 20:3; Deut 5:7) is the commandment given at the making of the first covenant. And just before his death, Moses says, "I have set before you life and death, blessing and curse; therefore choose life . . . loving the LORD your God, obeying his voice, and cleaving to him" (Deut 30:19–20). "I am the LORD, that is my name; my glory I give to no other, nor my praise to graven images" (Isa 42:8). This kind of exclusivity is not popular in today's culture. But it is the kind of relationship with his people that God has always insisted on having. So it is perhaps not too surprising that when Jesus comes, people must make a choice about him.

Before we go further, we must discuss John's use of the phrase "the Jews." It is sometimes said that John uses "the Jews" to refer to Jesus' unbelieving opponents because he blames the entire Jewish people for the death of Jesus. This has led to allegations that John is anti-Semitic. Scholars have discussed this issue a great deal, and we cannot discuss it fully here. But I will make a few points. John does not always use "the Jews" in a negative way. He sometimes uses it in a positive way (John 4:9, 22; 11:45; 12:11), and sometimes in a neutral way (John 2:6). Because John uses this phrase in a variety of ways, many scholars put "the Jews" in quotation marks in their discussions. For our purposes, it is sufficient to note that in John's Passion narrative, "the Jews" refers to those Jewish leaders who do not believe in Jesus (remembering that some do believe, such as Nicodemus and Joseph of Arimathea; and see John 12:42).

Let us return to John's story of Jesus' Roman trial. The first part of this story (John 18:28–32) takes place outside. "The Jews" bring Jesus to the praetorium, that is, the governor's official Jerusalem residence (normally Roman governors resided in Caesarea Maritima, but they would come to Jerusalem on feast days, to be personally on hand in case of trouble. Pilate has come up to be nearby for Passover). This was probably the former Palace of Herod. "The Jews" refuse to enter the praetorium, for fear of becoming ceremonially unclean at Passover time. So Pilate comes out to them, thus beginning to give in to their pressure. It is ironic that they are concerned about missing Passover, but are taking steps to sacrifice Jesus, the true Passover (John 1:29, 35; 1 Cor 5:7).

It is interesting that Jesus' Roman trial takes place in the praetorium, which may be considered Roman territory. First, this means that Jesus meets Pilate on Pilate's own turf, as it were. Just as he goes to Samaria and there meets the Samaritan woman and her townspeople (John 4:1–42), and goes to preach to his own people "in synagogues and the temple, where all Jews come together" (John 18:20), so he goes to the praetorium and meets Pilate. He does not seek these people out, but he puts himself where they can find him, if they seek him positively. Second, the praetorium is the place where Pilate should have the most power. So it is ironic that the praetorium is the place where he loses that power and gives in to "the Jews."

Pilate opens the trial by asking that the charge against Jesus be read out. "The Jews" are vague about the charge against Jesus, for reasons which will become clear later. So Pilate tells them either to give him a charge that is within his jurisdiction, or to deal with the case themselves. They are not to waste his time! He thinks that this is a mere religious quarrel among the Jews, since no one has told him that it is anything else, and he is not interested. "The Jews" remind Pilate that they have no authority to execute anyone. In a historical sense, they are talking about the Roman policy that if someone is sentenced to death by a local court, the Romans have reserved for themselves the right to carry the sentence out. This means that they can revoke the sentence if they choose, to protect locals who collaborate with them. But John sees something else happening as well: Jesus' predictions as to the manner of his death are being fulfilled (John 8:28; 12:32–33). In our study of this first part of the Passion narrative, we have seen the Scriptures being fulfilled. Here we see Jesus' own word being fulfilled, just as surely as the Scriptures. This is no surprise to the reader of the Gospel of John, who has read that Jesus himself is the Word of God (John 1:1) as much as the Scriptures are, and that the Scripture cannot be broken (John 10:35). Again we see that in spite of appearances, Jesus is the one who is really in charge of events.

2. Why is it important that Jesus die by the Roman method of crucifixion, rather than the Jewish method of stoning (for a hint, see Deut 21:22-23; Gal 3:13)?

Deut 21:22-23 refers to executing a man by stoning and then hanging his body from a tree branch, displaying the body to discourage others from committing crimes. Being hanged brings one under God's curse. By the first century, this verse was being applied to those executed by hanging from a wooden cross in crucifixion. So Paul does not hesitate to apply it to Jesus. God ordained in the law that a hanged person is under his curse because he knew ahead of time that Jesus would die by crucifixion. He ordained that Jesus would die in a way that would bring on him all the curses that come upon those who break the law (Deut 28:15-68). Those curses should have fallen on us, because none of us has kept God's law properly. All of us have sinned, and come up short of God's glorious ideal (Rom 3:23). But God loves us, and he does not want our sin to come between us and him. So he sent his Son Jesus to take on himself the sin that actually was ours. "God made him who had no sin to be sin for us, so that in him we might become the righteousness of God" (2 Cor 5:21 NIV). "All we like sheep have gone astray; we have turned every one to his own way; and the LORD has laid on him the iniquity of us all" (Isa. 53:6).

There is also a theological point here: God's plan for the salvation of the world is being carried out by those who do not recognize the significance of their actions. "The Jews" think that they are purging Israel of a heretic; Pilate thinks that he is thwarting a would-be revolutionary. Neither knows that God is using them to carry out his purposes, or what those purposes are. In the Old Testament, God makes similar use of Cyrus the Great, king of Persia (559-30 BC). Cyrus was not a worshipper of the God of Israel. But his conquest of the Babylonian Empire was God's judgment on Babylon for the way that Babylon had treated Israel (Isa 41:1-4, 25; 44:28; 45:1-7, 13; Jer 25:12-14). And his policy of religious tolerance toward the peoples that he conquered meant that the exiled Israelites could return home and rebuild the temple (Ezra 1:1-4).

DAY TWO

Not of This World
Today's key verses: John 18:33–40

Yesterday we began studying Jesus' Roman trial. We saw that John tells his story of the trial like a drama with seven scenes, and looked at the first scene. Today we will look at the second and third scenes. Please read John 18:33–38. Pilate has been outside talking to "the Jews." In verse 33 he goes inside to speak to Jesus. His question, "Are you the king of the Jews?" (18:33), presupposes that "the Jews" have phrased their charge to Pilate in this political manner (John does not record this, but see Luke 23:2, "We found this man perverting our nation, and forbidding us to give tribute to Caesar, and saying that he himself is Christ a king"). They know that Pilate will not deal with a religious matter, since it is not in his jurisdiction (compare Gallio's attitude in Acts 18:14–15). Pilate is in effect asking how Jesus pleads, Guilty or Not Guilty. Jesus answers by calling on Pilate to judge the evidence for himself, objectively, rather than being influenced by Jesus' opponents. In the Greek, Pilate's reply is phrased as if he expects the answer No. The best English translation would be, "I am not a Jew, am I?". Pilate is asking whether Jesus is a political king, which is what one would expect a Roman to ask.

3. What is ironic about Pilate's saying that he is not a Jew?

Ethnically, Pilate is a Roman. He is not a Jew, nor would he appreciate being called a Jew, a member of a conquered race. But in opposing Jesus, he joins himself with "the Jews," who oppose Jesus (tomorrow we will see a literary technique that John uses to connect the Romans and "the Jews"). For Pilate, since the leaders of Jesus' own people have turned him over to Pilate, Jesus must have committed some crime. All that Pilate wants to know is what Jesus has done. He has already made up his mind that Jesus is guilty.

In verse 36 Jesus says that his kingdom is not of this world. What does this mean? his kingdom (that is, his kingly activity in the world) is not of this world, any more than he is of this world (John 8:23). In other words, it does not have its origin, or its power source, in this world. Jesus is the Father's Emissary, acting in the world on the Father's behalf and carrying out the Father's orders (John 4:34; 5:19–23, 30; 6:38; 12:49; 14:10; 17:4). This close relationship with the Father is the source of Jesus' power and authority. So Jesus' kingdom has its origin in God, who is its power source. The citizens of Jesus' kingdom are his disciples, who draw their power from him the same way that he draws his power from God, and branches draw their power from the vine (John 15:1–8).

If Jesus' kingdom were of this world, he says, his servants, the citizens of his kingdom, would have fought to prevent his arrest (Peter's brief swordplay does not count as fighting, because Jesus did not approve it). They did not fight, which is an indication that there is a difference between Jesus' kingdom and Caesar's kingdom, which Pilate represents. The Greek word translated "servants" is *hyperetai*, the same word used for the temple attendants who have helped arrest Jesus. But Jesus does not have any servants of that kind. He calls his disciples friends (John 15:15), and they obey him because they love him (John 14:15, 23; 15:14), just as Jesus obeys the Father out of love (John 14:10). He calls them friends because Jesus' kingdom is based on love, while Caesar's kingdom is based on fear. But Pilate does not understand any of this. He cannot understand the idea of a kingdom that does not have its origin in this-worldly politics. He hears Jesus use the word "kingdom" and assumes that Jesus is speaking politically. It is as if he does not hear the phrase "not of this world." We may note that he does not ask, "What do you mean, not of this world?".

Jesus' kingdom is not of this world. But that does not mean that it is not active in this world, or that it is not concerned about it. We saw last week that God loves the world, and sent his Son into the world for its salvation. So what does this mean for us who are Jesus' disciples and friends in the world? If our Master's kingdom is active in, and concerned about, this world, so must we be. He could simply do everything by direct, miraculous intervention; and sometimes that is what he does. But that is not how he usually works. As it has often been said, he calls on us to be his hands and feet, acting for him in the world.

"You say that I am a king" (John 18:37) is partially affirmative: *You are right to say that I am a king. But I am not the kind of king that you are accustomed to.* Having told Pilate that he is not a political King, Jesus tells Pilate what he came into the world for: "to bear witness to the truth" (verse 37). Jesus has come into the world to proclaim the truth about God's saving activity in the world. He is uniquely qualified to do this because he has come down from heaven. He alone has seen God, so he is able to tell us all about him (John 1:18). Jesus tells Pilate, "Everyone who is of the truth hears my voice," that is, everyone who is of the truth understands and obeys Jesus' teaching. By implication, Jesus is inviting Pilate to be one of those who are of the truth. But Pilate is not interested. He replies sarcastically, "What is truth?" and leaves without waiting for an answer. He is frustrated, and understandably so. He is trying to hold a trial here! But "the Jews" are being evasive, and Jesus is speaking in riddles. Pilate is trying to get at the truth (meaning, the facts of the case), but no one is giving him straight answers to his straight questions. Because Pilate does not wait for an answer, that encourages the reader to answer the question. The reader knows that Jesus has already answered Pilate's question (John 14:6). That answer is, quite literally, standing right in front of Pilate.

So where do we go for truth? There are so many voices clamoring to be heard today that it can be difficult to choose which one to listen to. The many voices of the media, secular-humanistic psychology, and false religion all compete for our attention. We must be careful to listen only to Jesus, who himself is the truth, and to the Word of God, which is also truth (John 17:17). If we look anywhere else, we will find only falsehood, and the destruction which comes from falsehood. The devil is the source of all falsehood (John 8:44), and his only intention for humans is to destroy them (1 Pet 5:8). Our only protection is to get God's truth into our hearts and minds. It is no coincidence that truth is an important part of the armor of God (Eph 6:14).

4. Please read John 3:1–15. How does Pilate compare/contrast with Nicodemus?

Nicodemus is a leader of the Jews, probably a member of the Sanhedrin. As such, it is part of his job to investigate any man who claims to be a teacher from God. And he has taken the first step toward faith in Jesus. "No one can do these signs that you do, unless God is with him (John 3:2)." Like Pilate, Nicodemus is a man with a high place in society, a place which he may lose if he believes in Jesus. Nicodemus does not understand what Jesus says about spiritual birth, any more than Pilate understands what Jesus says about his kingdom. But Nicodemus keeps asking questions, because he wants to understand. Pilate asks no questions, which shows that he does not want to understand.

Please read John 18:38–40. Here is narrated the incident of Barabbas; Pilate has gone back outside. He tells "the Jews" that he finds no case against Jesus. He has not understood what Jesus has said, but he does understand that Jesus is not plotting to overthrow the Romans. Here Pilate's weakness becomes clearer. He has the authority to drop the case, but is too afraid of "the Jews" to do it. So he tries to get around them by means of the Passover amnesty. But he badly misjudges them, in that he fails to anticipate their reaction. About Barabbas, John says only that he is a bandit. The Greek word is *lestes*, "a man who attacks others and robs them with violence." It is the same word that Jesus uses of those who came before him, who enter the sheepfold by another way than the door (John 10:1, 8). The other Gospels tell us more about Barabbas. Barabbas is a violent man, in prison for attempting to overthrow the Romans, and for murder (Mark 15:7; Matt 27:16; Luke 23:18–19). He really is what Jesus is falsely accused of being! He is also the last man whom Pilate wants out on the streets, especially at a volatile time like Passover. So why does Pilate offer to release a man like that? Maybe he is astute enough to realize that the Jewish authorities do not want Barabbas on the streets either (for the reason, see John 11:48; they would be concerned about Roman reaction to any revolutionary). Maybe Pilate figures that given a choice between Jesus and Barabbas, they will choose Jesus to be released. If so, he has underestimated how much "the Jews" hate Jesus. This hatred may explain why "the Jews" are willing to choose the undesirable Barabbas over Jesus. They hate him so much that even Barabbas is preferable to him. No Gospel writer openly addresses this issue, nor the question of why no one speaks up for Jesus. People may be too afraid of "the Jews" to speak up (compare John 9:22; 12:42). Perhaps the best answer to these questions is that it was God's plan for Jesus to die. God set up the earthly circumstances which would allow his will to be carried out. God's plan for the salvation for the world is being carried out, in a way that even those involved never imagined.

DAY THREE

King of Thorns and Purple
Today's key verses: John 19:1–8

Today we will study the middle part, and climax, of John's story of Jesus' Roman trial. Please read John 19:1–3. Back inside, the Roman soldiers abuse and mock Jesus. Last week we saw the Jewish authorities mock Jesus as Prophet and Messiah; today we will see how the Romans mock him as King. These verses, where soldiers of the occupying power mock Jesus as a would-be "king of the Jews," are the centerpiece of the Roman trial scene. The soldiers do more than they know, because Jesus really is a King, of Gentiles as well as Jews. He is just not the kind of king that the world expects, because his kingdom is not of this world.

Verse 1 says, "Then Pilate took Jesus and scourged him." The phrasing fastens responsibility on Pilate as the commander who gives the order to his men. Flogging was part of the punishment of crucifixion, but Jesus has not yet been convicted. Pilate says that Jesus is innocent, but treats him as if he is guilty. Why Pilate orders that Jesus be flogged is not certain. If he thinks that flogging Jesus will satisfy the desire of "the Jews" to have Jesus punished, or will make them pity him, he has misjudged them again.

Flogging was an expected part of the sentence of crucifixion. But the reader sees something else happening as well. The soldiers' treatment of Jesus fulfills prophecy: "But he was wounded for our transgressions, he was bruised for our iniquities; upon him was the chastisement that made us whole, and with his stripes we were healed" (Isa 53:5). It was all for us! Jesus took the blows from that Roman whip so that we could be healed. Sickness and death came into the world as a result of sin. But at Calvary Jesus undid the results of sin by taking that sin on himself. So we can have healing for whatever ails us, physically and spiritually.

After the flogging, the soldiers engage in some rough horseplay with their prisoner, something that happens all too frequently when soldiers of an occupying power deal with members of a conquered race. Pilate has not authorized this, so responsibility for it falls on the soldiers. All the Romans have a share in the guilt for the death of Jesus. If this fellow wants to be king of the Jews, then they will dress him like a king! Or at least, what they do seems at first glance like horseplay. The believing reader may see something more in play.

A king must have a crown, so the soldiers take a few branches from a nearby thorn-bush and weave them into a wreath for Jesus' head. Thorns have significance in Scripture. They first appear in Gen 3:18: because of human sin, the ground will produce thorns and thistles. In Isa 5:6, God says what will happen to his vineyard (which represents Israel), because although he has tended it diligently, it has not borne the right fruit. "I will make it waste; it shall not be pruned or hoed, and briers and thorns shall grow up." And in Jer 4:3–4, God calls the people to come back to him: "Break up your fallow ground, and sow not among thorns. Circumcise the foreskin of your hearts, O men of Judah and inhabitants of Jerusalem." In Jer 12:13, God says of sinful Israel, "They have sown wheat and have reaped thorns, they have tired themselves out but profit nothing" (thorns are also associated with sin in Mic 7:4; Isa 32:13; Heb 6:8).

But thorns are not just a symbol of sin. Ezek 28:24 says, "And for the house of Israel there shall be no more a brier to prick or a thorn to hurt them among all their neighbors who have treated them with contempt." Here thorns are associated with being treated with contempt. Given these associations, it is no coincidence that Jesus wore a crown of thorns. He wore our sin and shame on his head as he went to the cross.

But that is not the end of the story. Ezek 28:24 predicts a time when there will be no more thorns. And Isa 10:17 says, "The light of Israel will become a fire, and his Holy One a flame; and it will burn and devour his thorns and briers in one day." In its context, this is a promise that after God has used the king of Assyria to deal with Israel for her unfaithfulness, he will deal with the king of Assyria for his pride and arrogance. But I suggest that beyond this immediate meaning, this verse also holds a promise that God will bring all sin to an end. He kept that promise when Jesus wore a crown of thorns.

Having given their mock-king a crown of thorns, the soldiers give him a royal robe. Most likely one of them throws his military cloak around Jesus' shoulders. These cloaks varied in shade according to the owner's rank. And different people can use different words for the same color: the jeans that I am wearing as I write this could be called "blue," or "denim," or "overdyed." And I once had a dress that I described as "blue-green," but my mother called it "sea green," and someone else said "sea blue." So there is no difficulty with John's (and Mark's) calling the "robe" purple (the color of royalty) while Matthew calls it scarlet. In a macabre case of adding insult to injury, the soldiers finish their mockery by approaching Jesus (Matthew adds that they kneel; Matt 27:29) and saying, "Hail, King of the Jews!" This is a parody of the homage by which they saluted the emperor, "Hail Caesar."

But there is more. In John 19:3 the Roman soldiers slap Jesus. This is similar to 18:22, where a temple attendant slaps him. And in John 18:38, Jesus says to Pilate, "Everyone who is of the truth hears my voice." This is similar to John 10:27, "My sheep hear my voice." Here he is talking to "the Jews," who should be his sheep. Both Pilate and "the Jews" decline the invitation. In this way John links the Romans with the Jewish leaders as enemies of Jesus. It is often said that John whitewashes the Romans to make the Jewish authorities, or the entire Jewish people, entirely guilty of the death of Jesus. But rather John makes both groups look equally guilty. John does not let "the Jews" off the hook in Jesus' death, but he does not let the Romans off the hook either.

Please read John 19:4–8. Outside once again, Pilate tells "the Jews" a second time that he finds no case against Jesus.

5. What is significant about the fact that in John 19:5, John says that Jesus "came out," not that he "was led out"?

That he comes out suggests that he is coming of his own free will. In other words, even in this condition—bruised, bleeding, and humiliated—he is the one who is in control of events. No matter how bad the circumstances look, Jesus is in charge.

6. If Jesus is in charge throughout his Passion, how does this apply to us?

This is good news for our lives as well. Jesus is as much in charge in our circumstances as he was in his own circumstances during his Passion. Even if the circumstances are beyond our control, they are not beyond God's control. Even Satan cannot attack us without God's permission (Job 1:12; 2:6; Luke 22:31). God will not allow our circumstances to destroy us, no matter how bad they seem to be. What is allowed will always be for our good and God's glory, even if it does not feel very comfortable.

Pilate's famous "Behold the man" has several possible meanings. It could be an expression of pity ("Look at the poor fellow"). Or maybe Pilate is impressed by Jesus' courage and dignity, and means, "Here is a real man." Whatever he means, Pilate is saying more than he knows. In one sense, he means that Jesus is not a political threat. All that unbelief can see is a bruised and bleeding mock-king. But in another sense, the reader sees that the Son of man is being lifted up, as he predicted (John 3:14; 8:28; 12:32). Whatever Pilate intends by showing Jesus to "the Jews" in this battered condition, it backfires, and they call for Jesus' crucifixion. He replies sarcastically, "Take him yourselves and crucify him!" He is not giving them permission to crucify Jesus. Rather he is daring them to exceed their authority and see how he will react when they themselves crucify a man whom he has pronounced innocent. They call on Pilate to respect their laws (Rome expected provincial governors to respect local laws, as long as they did not contradict Roman law). In doing so, they finally reveal the real reason that they want Jesus dead, which is not political: "He has made himself the Son of God." This is the thing which has angered "the Jews" throughout Jesus' ministry (John 5:18; 10:33). They have not wanted to tell Pilate this openly. But Pilate has forced their hand by not convicting Jesus out of hand. In another sense, the reader knows that earlier, "the Jews" ask Jesus who he is making himself out to be (John 8:53). But Jesus has not made himself anything. His power and authority come from the Father (John 5:19–23, 26–27; 8:54).

Pilate would not understand the phrase "Son of God" as a Jew would, but would think of the many stories in Greco-Roman mythology of the gods' offspring by human women. He would understand that Jesus has claimed to be some sort of divine being—and that he has shown Jesus little respect. This is why he is "even more afraid" (19:8): he is already afraid of the Jewish leaders (tomorrow we will see why), and now he becomes afraid of Jesus as well. He is trying to avoid making a choice about Jesus, but he will not be able to avoid it much longer. What will he do? The choice which he must make is the choice which every person must make. We must choose for Jesus or against him. What will we do?

DAY FOUR

Pilate's Choice
Today's key verses: John 19:9–16

Today we will look at the last two scenes of John's story of Jesus' Roman trial. Please read John 19:9–11. Pilate has been told that Jesus has claimed some sort of divinity. Alarmed, he goes back inside to investigate further. He asks Jesus, "Where are you from?" (verse 9). The question is deeper than he realizes. Jesus does not answer, because the complete answer is one that Pilate cannot understand. Where Jesus is from is a key question in the Gospel of John. Various Jews also discuss where Jesus is from, in John 7:41–42; 9:29–30. But they cannot understand a complete answer any more than Pilate can. In John 7:41–42, some people say that Jesus is the Christ. "But others said, 'Is the Christ to come from Galilee? Has not the Scripture said that the Christ is descended from David, and comes from Bethlehem, the village where David was?'" John seems to assume that the reader knows that Jesus was born in Bethlehem. But the reader also knows that the question of whether Jesus was born in Nazareth or Bethlehem is not as important as the question of whether Jesus is from God or not. This is what the Pharisees are discussing in John 9:29–30. They think that Jesus cannot be from God because he does not keep the Sabbath (John 9:16), and therefore is a sinner.

The crowd say in John 7:27 that they know where Jesus is from. For them, this is part of the problem: "We know where this man comes from; and when the Christ appears, no one will know where he comes from." In ancient Mediterranean societies, where a man is from is such an important part of his identity that it is often used as part of his name (e.g. Jesus *of Nazareth*; Joseph *of Arimathea*). Jesus knows where he is from: he has come from God (John 13:1). Knowing where he is from is part of Jesus knowing who he is. And because he knows who he is, he can face the ordeals of his Passion and overcome.

It is the same for us. Knowing who we are in Christ is key to facing and overcoming our trials. If we know and believe what God says about us, we will be better able to endure when other voices tell us something different. There are many Scriptures that tell us who we are in Christ. Several excellent writers have published lists of these Scriptures. If this is an issue for you, I encourage you to find these Scriptures and appropriate them into your heart and mind. This is the only cure for the insecurity which cripples so many Christians, especially women. Do not allow Satan to tell you that you are the only one with this problem. That is one of his lies, and isolation is one of his best weapons against us.

> 7. **If you struggle with insecurity, or with your identity in Christ, you are not alone. Why not ask someone in the group to pray with you?**

When Jesus does not answer Pilate's question (John 19:9), Pilate begins to bluster about the power he has. He is blustering because he is afraid: has Jesus' silence made him even more afraid than he already was? In one sense he is correct: as prefect, he has the authority to sentence Jesus to the cross or to drop the charges and release him. And this is where he is to blame in the situation. Instead of using his authority to prevent an injustice, he tries to use more oblique means, in hopes of avoiding the responsibility that comes with authority. And in so doing, he ends up abetting the injustice which he is trying to prevent.

In verse 11 Jesus tells Pilate, "He who handed you over to me has the greater sin." It has been said that in this saying John lays the blame for Jesus' death squarely on the Jewish people. But this is not so. Pilate may have the lesser sin, but he is still guilty. His sin is the lesser because as a Roman, he has not had the Scriptures, by which he could have recognized Jesus for who he is. For this reason Pilate's sin is less than that of the individual who handed Jesus over to him. But who is this? I suggest that this individual is Judas, who more than any other character in this Gospel is associated with handing over/ betraying (the Greek word is the same; John 6:71; 12:4).

Please read John 19:12-16. Back outside, Pilate continues to try to set Jesus free. But "the Jews" say, "If you let this man go, you are not Caesar's friend; every one who makes himself a king sets himself up against Caesar" (verse 12). In other words, if Pilate does not convict Jesus, they will tell the emperor that Pilate allowed an accused revolutionary to go free—something which Tiberius Caesar would hardly tolerate. This is the root of Pilate's weakness and fear of the Jewish leaders. If they report him, he will suffer the consequences (something which did happen a short time later, over another incident). "Caesar's friend" may have been a title conferred by the emperor on certain close associates, and Pilate may have held this title. Even if not, Pilate, as prefect appointed by the emperor, has a commitment to Caesar. Caesar is his patron, and he is Caesar's client. It is his duty to uphold Caesar's rule in the area under his jurisdiction. If he lets Jesus go, he will be failing in his duty, which would be dishonorable as well as risky.

Pilate now has no choice left. Rather than risk bringing Caesar's wrath down upon himself, he capitulates. This is consistent with the historical records: if the Jewish leaders stood up to Pilate on any issue, he tended to give in. For example, when the Jews protested because Pilate sent soldiers into Jerusalem carrying standards (the Roman equivalent of regimental flags) with images of Caesar on them, Pilate removed the standards. And a few years later, Pilate set up in the praetorium gold-coated shields with an inscription in honor of Caesar on them (the inscriptions probably read, "Tiberius Caesar, son of the *divine* Augustus," which would have upset Jews). When the Jewish leaders complained to Tiberius, Pilate moved the shields to Caesarea.

Bringing Jesus out, Pilate says to "the Jews," "Behold your king!" It is a last gesture of contempt and frustration against those who have outmaneuvered and shamed him. Considerations of honor and shame were very important in ancient Mediterranean societies. Pilate cannot allow himself to be "one-upped" by these people whom he is supposed to be governing. So he shows them what he thinks of their national hopes by showing them that the best king they can produce is a mock-king. They, predictably, are furious, and will have nothing to do with such a king. Here Pilate manages to salvage some political gain from the affair, because just as they have maneuvered him into convicting a man whom he knows is innocent, he maneuvers them into affirming their allegiance to Caesar. In a deeper sense, Jesus is the King who comes into His kingship precisely by way of his humiliation and suffering.

John does not record the words of a death sentence, but a formal sentence is implied by Pilate's sitting on the judgment seat. Under Roman law, a judge could walk around during a trial, but he was required to sit on the judgment seat while pronouncing the verdict and the sentence. It is also implied by the word "hand over" (Greek *paradidomi*), a legal technical term for remanding a prisoner into custody for carrying out of the sentence. In a deeper sense, the roles are reversed: even as Pilate judges Jesus, he brings down judgment on himself by his choice. By affirming their allegiance to Caesar, "the Jews" repudiate the Scriptural declaration that God alone is King of Israel (see, e.g., 1 Sam 8:7; 10:19; Pss 5:2; 10:16; Isa 33:22; 43:15). It is especially ironic that they would say this at Passover, because one of the traditional Passover hymns ends, "Lord, we have no king but you."

There is an issue which you may have noticed that I have not mentioned, but which sometimes arises when this passage is discussed. That issue is politics (defined as Roman-Jewish relations). In recent years, it has been trendy to see Pilate as the big, bad Roman who tramples on the oppressed Jews. According to this view, Pilate's aim throughout the trial is to make "the Jews" admit allegiance to Caesar. But I suggest that John's text does not support this interpretation.

First, we may notice that it is not Pilate who is in control but "the Jews," and that right from the beginning of the trial, when they make Pilate come out to them by refusing to go inside to him. Second, I do not see any indications from the text that Pilate's intention from the start is to ridicule Jewish national hopes. New Testament scholar Raymond Brown says rightly that "Pilate's attempt to salvage political gain from the affair is by petulant afterthought."[1] It is his revenge for their humiliating him by forcing him to condemn a man against his will and his better judgment. Rather, his intention is to avoid making a choice. In general I suggest that the emphasis in the encounter between Jesus and Pilate is on Pilate's response to Jesus rather than any issue of Roman-Jewish relations. As we saw on Day One of this week, what is important in this passage is the choice which Pilate must make about Jesus. Because he refuses to take a stand for Jesus, he is forced to take a stand against him. Warren Wiersbe notices a pattern in the passages which we have studied this week and last week. He says that Pilate gives in to the world, Peter gives in to the flesh, and Judas gives in to the devil.[2]

This is not to say that this encounter is entirely lacking in political overtones. If one's allegiance is to the King whose kingdom is not of this world, it cannot also be to Caesar, or any other king whose kingdom is of this world. So there is a sense in which Pilate must choose between Jesus and Caesar. But what is important in this encounter is Pilate's choice, not politics.

1. *Death*, 1:753 note 45.
2. *Be Loyal*, 253.

8. Have you ever been pressured to do something that you knew was not right? If it is appropriate, why not share with the group?

It is not too difficult to see how this issue of choice applies to our lives. Just as the characters in the Gospel of John have to make a choice about Jesus, so do we. The most important way in which this choice appears is our choice to accept or reject God's offer of salvation through faith in Jesus. But for us who accept that offer, it does not end there. Every day we must choose to do what is right in God's eyes or what is not. Sometimes we must choose whether to take a stand that is in line with God's Word on a given issue, or one that is popular with the world. We cannot sit on the fence, any more than Pilate can. Anyone who is not for Jesus is against him (Matt 12:30).

DAY FIVE

Buffoonery, Water, and Blood
Today's key verses: Luke 23:6–12; Matt 27:19, 24–25

We must look briefly at three incidents connected with Jesus' Roman trial which John does not record. Luke records one, and Matthew the other two. Please read Luke 23:6–12. Pilate, finding out from the Jewish authorities that Jesus is from Galilee, sends him to Herod, the ruler of Galilee (this is Herod Antipas, son of Herod the Great). Why does Pilate send Jesus to Herod? Perhaps he sees Herod's presence as a chance to get rid of the case. Perhaps he sees an opportunity to mend fences with Herod. Apparently there has been a violent incident of some kind involving some Galileans at the temple (Luke refers to it briefly at Luke 13:1; the details are unknown to us, but Luke seems to assume that his readers know what he is talking about). So Pilate may welcome a chance to smooth things over (if only to keep himself out of trouble, as we discussed yesterday). Herod, meanwhile, is eager to see Jesus, because he has heard of him and wants to see a sign from him. From mentions earlier in this Gospel, we may guess that Herod is not entirely motivated by curiosity. In Luke 9:7–9, Herod believes that Jesus can do miracles because he is John the Baptist raised from the dead. Since Herod is the one who had John executed, it would not be surprising if he were afraid as well as curious. In Luke 13:31–33, some Pharisees warn Jesus that Herod is after him (why do they warn him? Luke does not say. Perhaps these Pharisees, unlike most, are favorable to him; compare John 12:42–43). We may note that Jesus takes the warning seriously. He calls Herod a fox (a creature known in Israelite society for its destructiveness; Song 2:15; Ezek 13:3–4). This suggests that Herod's fear of Jesus has led to defensiveness and hostility toward him.

This fear may partially explain why Herod wants to see a sign from Jesus: a sign will prove who Jesus is. So Herod approaches Jesus with mixed motives: a desire to find out whether his fears are justified, and a desire to be entertained. But Jesus will not respond to anyone who comes to him with either of these ideas in mind.

The chief priests and scribes follow Jesus into Herod's presence, and accuse him vehemently. But he does not answer their strident accusations, any more than he answers Herod's eager questions (we may note that he does answer the calmer Pilate). They want Herod to find Jesus guilty. But Herod, like Pilate, sees an opportunity to mend fences. So he sends Jesus back to Pilate, deferring to the prefect in the matter. In doing so, he also places the responsibility for Jesus' fate back onto Pilate. In fact Pilate cannot escape the responsibility, no matter how much he wants to. Even if Herod finds Jesus guilty, the death sentence must be confirmed by Pilate, and his soldiers must carry it out.

Before he sends Jesus back to Pilate, Herod vents his frustration with this unco-operative prisoner. If Jesus will not entertain him, he will use Jesus to entertain himself! He joins his soldiers in mocking Jesus, ending by dressing him in "gorgeous apparel" (verse 11). The Greek word translated "gorgeous" is *lampros*, which means "bright" or "shining." It is often used of white clothing, but not always. It suggests a royal robe. In other words, Herod mocks Jesus as King, as someone who wants to take Herod's place.

9. What is Jesus' view of faith based on signs (for a hint, see Luke 4:3–4, 9–12; 11:16, 29; John 2:23–25; 4:48)? Why?

In Luke 4, Satan encourages Jesus to perform signs as part of tempting him. In verse 3, the devil tells him to turn a stone into bread. Since he has eaten nothing for forty days, it would be understandable if he wanted to meet his physical needs. After all, his body was no different than ours! But miraculously-produced bread will only distract him from the spiritual nourishment provided by the Word of God (for a similar attitude toward food brought by the disciples, see John 4:31–34). It will also turn his focus from God onto himself (we need to avoid self-focus even more than he did).

In Luke 4:9–11, the devil urges Jesus to claim the promise of divine protection of Ps 91 and then jump from the height of the temple. Now, the promises of Ps 91 are for God's children to claim if God tells them to do something dangerous for him, such as being a missionary in a place that is hostile to Christianity. But Jesus knows that God is not obligated to protect him if he performs showy, risky stunts that God has not called him to do. The equivalent for us would be to claim these promises and then jump off a high building or a bridge, just to see if God will send an angel to catch us. That is putting God to the test, and no good will come of it.

In Luke 11:16 it is not the devil who is testing Jesus but the people, who are asking him for a sign from heaven. Jesus describes this as the act of "an evil generation" (Luke 11:29). They are demanding that Jesus give them positive proof that he is the Messiah before they will believe in him. Jesus calls this evil because it leaves no room for faith. This is believing by knowledge, not believing by faith.

Another reason that Jesus does not approve of faith based on signs is that this kind of faith is not secure enough to withstand disappointment. What happens when God does not perform on our cue? How do we react when God does not do what we want him to do, when we want him to do it? The only kind of faith which will not crumble when this happens is faith which is founded on trust in God rather than on signs.

We must also note that Satan and his agents are also capable of doing signs and wonders. We must be careful to discern which miracles come from God and which are false. We can only do this if we are grounded in God's written Word. This requires study and discipline, and it is not as easy as being entertained by watching someone else perform signs and wonders. But it is the only way to avoid being deceived. In general, signs and wonders are to confirm and support the written Word and godly preaching; they are not supposed to be the center of attention (Mark 16:20).

Let us return to Herod's encounter with Jesus. Having made fun of this Galilean who (he thinks) wants to replace him, Herod sends Jesus back to Pilate. The fence-mending operation is successful, because Herod and Pilate are friends from that time on (Luke 23:12). We may say that just as Jesus heals the ear of the high priest's servant (Luke 22:51), so he heals the conflict between Herod and Pilate. Luke in his Passion narrative stresses that Jesus brings forgiveness and healing to his opponents, even in the midst of his own suffering. Thus he does has he told his disciples to do (Luke 6:35–36).

We must now look at two incidents from Jesus' Roman trial which Matthew alone records. Please read Matt 27:19, 24–25. In Matt 27:19, Pilate's wife sends her husband a message: he should have nothing to do with Jesus (whom she calls "that righteous man"), because she has had a bad dream about Jesus. It is close to the end of the trial, because Pilate is sitting on the judgment seat. He is about to deliver the verdict and the sentence. It may seem strange to modern readers that she would interrupt him during a trial with concerns about a dream. But the Romans took dreams seriously. Pilate would consider his wife's message an important one. It gives him another reason to believe that Jesus might be in some way divine (remember our discussion of John 19:8 on Day Three of this week), another reason besides the envy of the Jewish authorities (see Mark 15:10; Matt 27:18) to get rid of the case. That Pilate's wife should have such a dream does not mean that she is a believer in Jesus, or a convert to Judaism. Rather she is like the magi of Matt 2:1–12. Like them, she is a Gentile who is quicker to understand who Jesus is than Herod and the Jewish authorities, who, as Jews, should be the first to understand who Jesus is.

His wife's message makes Pilate all the more eager to be rid of the case. But the Jewish authorities are just as eager for Jesus' execution as Pilate is for his release. Finally, after their second outcry for crucifixion, Pilate has a bowl of water brought to him. He washes his hands, a symbolic gesture indicating his innocence in Jesus' death (Matt 27:24). The Jewish authorities, and Jewish readers of Matthew's Gospel, would understand this gesture (see Pss 26:6; 73:13; and especially Deut 21:6–8). So would Gentile readers of Matthew (Herodotus, *History* 1.35; Vergil, *Aeneid* 2.719; Sophocles, *Ajax* 654).

Pilate tells the crowd that if they insist on executing Jesus, they must take responsibility for his blood: "see to it yourselves." This is exactly the same thing that the Jewish leaders tell Judas when he confesses to having shed innocent blood: "see to it yourself" (Matt 27:4). The people are willing to do this: "His blood be on us and on our children!" (Matt 27:25).

Both Judas and Pilate try to avoid responsibility in Jesus' death; neither man can escape his share of it.

This verse, or rather its misuse, has been the cause of so much anguish that I approach it with trepidation. People have used it to justify their own anti-Semitism, and history, especially in the twentieth century, has shown what tragic results anti-Semitism can have. But to use this verse to justify "Christian" anti-Semitism is to use it in a way that was never intended.

Let us look at this verse in a way which is (hopefully) both honest and compassionate. First, we must admit that with this saying the Jews present at Jesus' trial take responsibility for his death. But does this mean that *all* the responsibility is to be placed on them? We have seen that as hard as Pilate tries to escape his share of the responsibility, he cannot. It is interesting that each of the later Evangelists, as he tells the story under the guidance of the Holy Spirit, expresses this idea in his own way. Matthew records Plate's handwashing gesture; Luke records that Pilate sends Jesus to Herod, who promptly sends him back. John, as we have seen this week, records Pilate's vacillation as he ping-pongs between Jesus and "the Jews." When they threaten to report him to Caesar, he has no choice but to give in. The Gospels make the Jews, especially their leaders, and the Romans equally responsible for Jesus' death.

We may also say that Matt 27:25 refers to the speakers and their children. Whatever responsibility is attributed to the Jews is limited to those two generations. It does not refer to any generation which has arisen since then. And let us remember that God has not abandoned Israel (Rom 9–11, especially 11:1–6, 17–32), and that if the Gentiles have salvation, it comes from the Jews (John 4:22). Jesus himself was a Jew, a fact which Matthew reflects in his genealogy of Jesus by beginning with Abraham (Matt 1:1). And Simeon calls Jesus "a light for revelation to the Gentiles and *for glory to thy [God's] people Israel*" (Luke 2:32, emphasis added).

10. If the crowd at the praetorium has Jesus' blood on them, what has Jesus already said about his blood?

Jesus has already said that his blood is "poured out for many for the forgiveness of sins" (Matt 26:28). So we can hardly say that there is no forgiveness for them. Above all, we must remember that all of us have sinned (Rom 3:23). No man, woman, or child ever born is without sin. That means that in a theological sense, each one of us is responsible for the death of Jesus.

As commentator Donald Hagner puts it, "it is sin, the universal malady of human beings, that drives Jesus to the cross. The crucifixion is in this sense a piece of the autobiography of every man and woman ever to walk this earth. It is 'I' who am guilty of crucifying Jesus."[3]

At this point Pilate turns Jesus over to his soldiers for crucifixion (John 19:16). It is the Day of Preparation for Passover, at around noon. The Jewish authorities did not want to arrest Jesus during the feast, in case the people rioted in protest (Mark 14:2). But God's timing overrules human planning. In the temple, it is time for the Passover lambs to be sacrificed. It is also time for the sacrifice of Jesus, the Lamb of God.

---

3. *Matthew 14–28*, 828.

WEEK 5

Via Dolorosa

DAY ONE

Carrying the Crossbeam
Key verses: Mark 15:21–32; Luke 23:27–31, 34, 39–43, 46;
John 19:19–30

V*IA DOLOROSA* ("SORROWFUL ROAD") is the Latin name which some parts of the church give to the route that Jesus took from the praetorium to the place where he was crucified. Our study this week begins on that route. Please read Mark 15:21–24. It was customary for a person condemned to crucifixion to carry the crossbeam (in Latin, the *patibulum*) of their cross to the execution site. Apparently Jesus is unable to carry his crossbeam all the way there, because the Roman soldiers conscript a passerby, Simon of Cyrene, to carry it (Cyrene was a city on what is now the northeastern coast of Libya, in the province that is still called Cyrenaica). The Greek word translated "compelled" is *angareuo*. It means "to compel someone to do military service." Matthew and Luke mention Simon (Matt 27:32; Luke 23:26), but only Mark mentions his sons. This is probably because Alexander and Rufus were known to Mark's first readers, but not Matthew's or Luke's. The Rufus mentioned here may be the same as the Rufus whom Paul mentions in Rom 16:13, but we cannot be certain of this, because Rufus was a fairly common name. Paul mentions an Alexander who opposes him (1 Tim 1:20; 2 Tim 4:14), and the name also appears in Acts 4:6 (this Alexander is a member of the high-priestly family, living in Jerusalem) and Acts 19:33 (this

Alexander is a Jew living in Ephesus, probably one who believes in Jesus, since he wants to defend Paul). Alexander was a very common name in the Greco-Roman world, so the New Testament could refer to as many as five different Alexanders. About Simon himself we know little. Simon is probably a Gentile, because he is traveling, which was not allowed for Jews on a feast day. Whoever he is, he probably became a Christian like his sons.

Please read Luke 23:27–31. Following Jesus is a crowd of people, including women who lament for him. He tells them that they should mourn not for him, but for themselves and their children. He warns them that a time is coming when those who are childless will be better off than those who have children, because tribulation is coming. He warns of tribulation by quoting part of Hosea 10:8. "The high places of Aven, the sin of Israel, shall be destroyed. Thorn and thistle shall grow up on their altars; and they shall say to the mountains, Cover us, and to the hills, Fall upon us." This verse warns that judgment is about to fall on the Northern Kingdom of Israel for her unfaithfulness to God. (It is also quoted in Rev 6:16–17, as all humanity realizes that "the great day of their [God's and the Lamb's] wrath has come, and who can stand before it?"). The prophecy Jesus makes was fulfilled when the Romans sacked Jerusalem in AD 70. Knowing the original context of this verse in Hosea helps us to understand the meaning of the fall of Jerusalem. Just as Israel's faithlessness leads to the conquest of Samaria by the Assyrians, so the refusal of the Jewish leaders to listen to Jesus will lead to God's judgment (something which Jesus mourns over in Luke 19:41–44). Jerusalem will fall to the Romans as surely as Samaria fell to the Assyrians.

Jesus' prophecy ends with a cryptic question: "If they do this when the wood is green, what will happen when it is dry?" (Luke 23:31). What does this mean? The most likely meaning is, if the Jewish leaders treat Jesus like this when the Romans are not forcing them to do so, how much worse will things get when the Romans themselves attack Jerusalem? The contrast between the green wood and the dry symbolizes the contrast between a favorable time and an unfavorable one.

The execution site is named in Hebrew *Golgotha*, in Greek *Kranion*, in Latin *Calvaria* (from which we get the name Calvary), in English, Skull. It was somewhere outside the city walls, near a road. Why was this place called Skull? Three answers have been suggested. The first is that it may have been a rounded hill, shaped like the top of a human head. The second is that it was called Skull simply because it was a place of execution, of death. The third is that there was a Jewish tradition that this was the place where Adam (or at least his skull) was buried. This would mean that the Last Adam dies where the First Adam died. This would be a neat and beautiful piece of symbolism. Unfortunately there is nothing in Scripture to support it. I suggest that the first answer is the most likely.

Please read John 19:19–22. Pilate has had a sign prepared, showing the charge against Jesus. It was customary for such a sign to be carried ahead of the condemned man, or hung around his neck, and placed on top of the cross, or in the ground near it. This sign reads, "Jesus of Nazareth, the king of the Jews." This wording does not please "the Jews," because it makes it sound as if they acknowledge Jesus as their king. But Pilate will not back down; he is finally ready to stand up to them.

1. **What is the significance of the fact that the sign is in three languages?**

The sign is in Aramaic, the language spoken by Jews in Palestine in the first century (it was similar to Hebrew, and used Hebrew letters); Latin, the official language of Rome, and Greek, the everyday language of the Mediterranean world. Pilate says more than he knows, because by using these languages he acknowledges Jesus as king of both Jews and Gentiles, including Pilate's own people.

At Golgotha, the soldiers offer Jesus wine mixed with myrrh. In the ancient world, wine perfumed like this was considered a delicacy, fit for royalty. This means that the soldiers are continuing to mock Jesus as a would-be king. It is sometimes said that they give Jesus wine to ease the pain of crucifixion, and that he refuses it because he chooses to experience fully the suffering that the Father has ordained for him (compare John 18:11) without his senses being artificially dulled. But that is not what is happening here. The giving of wine to those being crucified was a custom of the women of Jerusalem, based on Prov 31:6–7: "Give strong drink to him who is perishing, and wine to those in bitter distress; let them drink and forget their poverty, and remember their misery no more." But the women of Jerusalem are not mentioned at Golgotha. It is the Roman soldiers who give Jesus the wine, for their own reasons. Jesus endures their mockery as part of what is ordained for him, but he will not participate in it.

A word about crucifixion is in order at this point. Crucifixion was not only an extremely painful form of execution, it was also very humiliating. The Romans considered it too shameful for Roman citizens, and suitable only for slaves and foreigners. A man sentenced to death by crucifixion would be flogged after sentence had been pronounced, before carrying the crossbeam out to the execution site. The whip used, called a *flagellum*, was a sort of cat-o'-nine-tails, made of several leather braids with small metal balls or sharp pieces of bone braided in. Repeated blows with this would tear the skin through until often muscle, bones and even internal organs would be exposed. It is not surprising, then, that some men would die at this stage. A story that is told about the making of the film *The Passion of the Christ* is on point here. It is said that during the filming of the flogging scenes, a wooden board was placed against the back of actor James Caviezel, who played Jesus, so that he would not actually be struck by the *flagellum* (the camera was placed at such an angle that the board was not visible). But one time the actor playing the soldier missed the board and struck Caviezel. The pain from that single blow was so great that Caviezel fainted. One can only imagine what several dozen blows would feel like.

The Jewish law limited the number of lashes that a condemned person could receive to forty (Deut 25:3). By the first century AD, it had become customary to limit the number to thirty-nine, to avoid an accidental miscount (compare 2 Cor 11:24, where Paul says that he received this treatment on five occasions). The Romans, however, had no such rule. They would flog their prisoner until the soldier doing the flogging became too tired to continue.

The upright of the cross (in Latin, the *stipes*) would already be affixed in the ground at the execution site. The crossbeam and the condemned would be laid on the ground, and the condemned man's hands would be fastened to the crossbeam either by tying or by nails (which were 7 in./17.5 cm. long) through the wrists (the Greek word for "hand" can also include the wrist). During this process the arms would be stretched, often to the point of dislocating the shoulders. The crossbeam was then raised up and inserted into a notch cut into the upright, either at the top (which gave a T-shape) or at some distance below the top (which gave the shape that we accociate with the cross). The feet would be nailed to each side of the upright, a wooden plaque being placed against the outside of the heel before a nail was driven through both plaque and heel. A small piece of wood was sometimes attached to the upright, to be used as a support for the feet or buttocks while the crossbeam was being put into place. Death often took several days. When I think about the physical suffering that Jesus went through, for my sake and yours, I cannot help but be moved. And as we will see in the next few days, the physical suffering was only the beginning.

The Gospel writers, however, do not go into these gory details, probably because it was unnecessary. Today, when a criminal is executed, it is done within the walls and closed doors of a prison, with only those closest to the case as witnesses. But it was different in ancient times. Crucifixion was a very public event, intended to deter others from committing the same crime. The original readers of the Gospels would know the procedure. That is why the Evangelists are all so brief about the actual notice of Jesus' crucifixion. Raymond Brown says that the crucifixion of Jesus has been "more often portrayed in art than any other scene in history . . . Yet in all comparable literature, has so crucial a moment ever been phrased so briefly or uninformatively?"[1]

2. What does it mean to you that Jesus suffered so much for us?

Oh my Friend, if you ever feel unloved or unvalued, if you ever feel like you are in last place, look at Calvary. See what Jesus went through to redeem you from your sins! And we can only begin to imagine what the Father's heart felt as he turned away from his one and only, beloved Son as that Son died. Impossible that they would make such a sacrifice for someone whom they did not love and value more highly than words can express. The motto of a well-known cosmetics company is "Because you're worth it." If you feel like you have no worth or value, know that Jesus went to Calvary because you are worth it!

---

1. *Death*, 2:945.

DAY TWO

Forgiveness and Freedom
Today's key verses: Luke 23:34–39, 43;
John 19:23–24; Mark 15:27–32

Yesterday we took our first steps along the Via Dolorosa: we walked with Jesus from the praetorium to Calvary, and saw him crucified there. None of the Evangelists records all of the events that we will study this week and next, and we must combine the Gospels to get the whole picture. Luke records the first of what are sometimes called the "Seven Last Words From the Cross." Immediately after Jesus is crucified, he prays, "Father, forgive them, for they know not what they do" (Luke 23:34). Throughout his Gospel, Luke stresses Jesus' mercy and forgiving grace. These surely reach a climax in this prayer. In the midst of his suffering Jesus prays for those who are mistreating him, just as he has told his disciples to do (Luke 6:28). His prayer does not cover only the soldiers who have physically nailed him to the cross, but the Jewish leaders as well. It is clear enough why he can say that the Roman soldiers do not know what they are doing. They are Gentiles who know little about God. But how can he say that the Jewish leaders, who have read the Scriptures and heard Jesus preaching, do not know what they are doing? Even those who plan evil would not have acted as they did if they had known (i.e., appreciated God's goodness or understood his plan; compare Luke 19:42; Acts 3:17; 13:27; 1 Cor 2:8). As Raymond Brown sums it up, "If there were those who did not know because they have not been told, there were also those who, although they had been told, they had not grasped. It is noteworthy, however, that even though the latter group do not know what they are doing, they still need forgiveness."[2]

In this saying, as in so many other things, Jesus is our example. We must note that he forgives while he is being mistreated; he does not wait until the abuse is over. And because he forgave like this, so can we. My experience on the Prayer Lines has shown me that many people, even Christians, find it painfully difficult to forgive those who have hurt them, and many have been badly hurt by not forgiving. Was it a struggle for Jesus to forgive those who mistreated and mocked him? Did he have

---

2. *Death*, 2:973.

trouble forgiving? Probably not. But he understands when we do. And he will help us follow his example. In fact, he gives us a command to forgive, not just an example. The Lord's Prayer says, "forgive us our trespasses, as we forgive those who have trespassed against us." And Jesus follows this model prayer with a warning: "For if you forgive men their trespasses, your heavenly Father will also forgive you; but if you do not forgive men their trespasses, neither will your Father forgive your trespasses" (Matt 6:14–15). This gives us an idea of how seriously God takes this issue.

But God will not call on us to do something and then leave us without the power to obey. If there is someone whom you need to forgive, and you are having difficulty doing it, ask God to help you to release them to him in forgiveness. To do this is not to say that you were not hurt by what they did.[3] Nor is it to say that what the offender did to you is okay. But forgiving them will make you okay, because it will release you from the power of the hurt. Once that happens, then you can heal. And if we do not forgive, we leave an open door for Satan. Paul says that he forgives "to keep Satan from gaining the advantage over us; for we are not ignorant of his devices" (2 Cor 2:10–11). And again, "Do not let the sun go down on your anger, and do not give an opportunity to the devil" (Eph 4:26–27). Unforgiveness brings emotional destruction on ourselves and hampers our witness to others. It also blocks God from bringing good out of our suffering, which he wants to do (Rom 8:28). That is why God places such a high value on forgiveness and takes this issue so seriously. He does not want us to stay in this kind of bondage. It is interesting that the basic meaning of the Greek word for "forgive," *aphiemi*, is "release; let go." Forgiveness is a release that brings us release.

Please read John 19:23–24. Having secured Jesus to the cross, the Roman soldiers settle down to keep guard over him until he dies. They divide his clothes among themselves; it was customary for execution squads to receive the clothing of their prisoners, and being naked, or nearly naked, on the cross was part of the shame of crucifixion (the Romans usually crucified men naked. But it may be that in Judea men sentenced to crucifixion were allowed to wear a loincloth, as a concession to Jewish sensitivities about public nudity). But there is more to this than soldiers getting their usual perks for carrying out their duty. John mentions that

---

3. In this paragraph I am drawing on Moore, *Living*, 129.

the soldiers' actions fulfill Scripture (he quotes Ps 22:18). As we have seen before, God's will is being carried out through those who do not recognize the significance of their actions. Only John mentions Jesus' tunic, seamless and woven from top to bottom. Such a garment was valuable, so the soldiers throw dice for it instead of tearing it up. Since shortly after John's Gospel was written, preachers, scholars and writers have exercised their imaginations, looking for symbolism in this tunic. Some say that it symbolizes Jesus' high-priestly role. But the high priest's garment is a robe, not a tunic, and John does not stress the idea of Jesus as high priest. Some say that the tunic symbolizes the unity of the church and its origin in God. The problem here is that Jesus has had his tunic taken from him. Perhaps it is best to say that no symbolism is intended.

All the Gospels mention that two other men are crucified along with Jesus. They may have been accomplices of Barabbas, but this is not stated. None of the Gospel writers mentions the specific crime for which these men are executed, nor even their names (names for them were supplied by later tradition). All that is said about them is that they are positioned one on each side of Jesus, with Jesus in the middle, the position of honor. Thus Jesus, "the King who reigns from the wood," comes to his glory precisely through his shame and suffering. The reader may also be reminded of Mark 10:37-40, where James and John ask to be seated on either side of Jesus in his glory. Jesus answers that that is not for him to decide, but those positions are for those for whom they are prepared. Ironically, they are prepared for two unnamed criminals who are crucified on either side of Jesus' cross.

Please read Mark 15:27-32. Just as the Roman soldiers mock Jesus by giving him wine, so also some Jews mock him. Some passersby call on him to prove that he could have destroyed the temple and rebuilt it in three days (compare Mark 14:58-59) by coming down from the cross (we discussed the temple claim in Week 3). The chief priests and lawyers say, "He saved others; he cannot save himself." Here they say more than they know. They mean that he healed other people, but he cannot now save himself by coming down from the cross. But in a deeper sense, they are right. If Jesus is to save others, in the spiritual sense, he cannot save himself. He must give his life for the life of the world (John 6:51). If he is the Messiah, they say, let him prove it by coming down from the cross, so that they may see and believe. In other words, they are asking for signs again (we discussed faith based on signs last week). They do not understand that Jesus proves that he is the Messiah precisely by staying on the cross. They say that they will not believe unless they see. But Jesus calls down blessings on those who believe even though they have not seen (John 20:29; we will have more to say about this in Week 7). The passersby and chief priests in their mockery call on Jesus to come down from the cross because they do not think that he can actually do it. But they are wrong. Just as he chooses not to call for help from angels in Gethsemane (Matt 26:53–54), here on Calvary he chooses not to come down from the cross. As I read these verses I think, "What if he *had* come down?" My heart overflows with gratitude that he did not.

Please read Luke 23:39–43. At this point Luke turns his attention to the men crucified along with Jesus. At first these men have insulted Jesus along with the passersby and the chief priests (Mark 15:32). But at some point one of them has a change of heart. He rebukes the first criminal for not fearing God even in their present situation. He confesses Jesus' innocence and his own guilt, and asks Jesus to remember him when Jesus comes into his kingdom (thus he acknowledges Jesus as King). Jesus assures him that his request will be granted. Indeed we may say that it is more than granted. The criminal says, "Remember me;" Jesus says, in effect, "I will take you with me." The criminal says, "when you come into your kingdom;" Jesus says, "Today." In fact Jesus' own request is also being granted; his prayer of forgiveness (Luke 23:34) is answered by this man's repentance, and by the salvation of the centurion at the cross (Mark 15:39) and the growth of the church after Pentecost.

3. In Luke 23:39, what is the first criminal really asking Jesus?

In asking Jesus to save himself and them, the first criminal is asking Jesus to come down from the cross, and bring them with him. Interestingly, his question, "Are you not the Christ?" assumes that Jesus is the Messiah. The criminal expects that since Jesus is the Messiah, he will get them all out of their predicament. He does not understand that because he is the Messiah, Jesus must suffer. In other words, he is looking for immediate relief from his circumstances. He just wants the pain to go away! I have talked with many people on the Prayer Lines who make variations on this theme: "Pray that these neighbors will leave me alone!" "I wish my boss weren't so mean to me!" "I just want out of this marriage!" They want nothing more than to feel better. They just want God to change their circumstances. But sometimes God wants to change us. His goal is to make us spiritually mature, and if temporary earthly discomfort will accomplish that, he will use it. The second criminal, on the other hand, asks for eternal relief. He is prepared to let God use the circumstances to change him.

4. Has God ever used difficult circumstances to change you? If it is appropriate, why not share with the group?

We may also say that these two criminals illustrate the two possible ways that humans can respond to the cross of Jesus. The second criminal sees salvation in humiliation, the first cannot. This is the "stumbling block" which kept many Jews from believing in Jesus (Rom 9:32–33; 1 Cor 1:23; Gal 5:11). To them, the Messiah was to be a glorious military leader. A suffering Messiah seemed like a contradiction in terms. They did not understand that the Scriptures point to a servant-Messiah who would suffer for other people's sins, not his own. The criminals also illustrate salvation by grace. Pinned to their crosses, they can do nothing for themselves. All that they can do is to accept the forgiveness which Jesus offers them, or reject it. Only Jesus can help them. As Paul puts it, "by grace you have been saved through faith; and this is not your own doing, it is the gift of God—not because of works" (Eph 2:8–9).

DAY THREE

Darkness at Noon
Today's key verses: John 19:25–27; Mark 15:33–37

Please read John 19:25–27. Standing by Jesus' cross are four women: his mother; his mother's sister, whose name is not mentioned; another Mary, the wife of Clopas; and Mary Magdalene. These four women are contrasted with the soldiers (probably a squad of four) who crucify Jesus. They are also contrasted with the male disciples, who (with one exception) have gone into hiding.

John next reports a scene between Jesus, his mother, and the Beloved Disciple. It is a moment of tenderness in the midst of all the brutality and the insults. Here Jesus commends his mother and the Beloved Disciple to each other's care. It is interesting that no names are mentioned. These two people are known only by their connection to Jesus, as mother and disciple.

In an earthly sense, Jesus as eldest son is ensuring that his mother will be cared for [has the unbelief of his brothers (John 7:5) caused a rift in the family?]. But many have also seen this scene as symbolic, seeing Jesus' mother as the New Eve, mother of the church. Others have seen her as representing Jewish Christianity, while the Beloved Disciple represents Gentile Christianity which adopts Jewish Christians into the church. But it is seems unlikely that such symbolism is intended. Rather it is best to interpret this scene in light of the only other appearance of Jesus' mother in John's Gospel, in John 2:1–11. There she asks him to deal with a shortage of wine at a wedding. But he demurs, placing the Father's timing ahead of earthly family connections. She must come to him on the basis of faith, like anyone else. Here at the cross she does exactly that, taking her place with other disciples. The reader may be reminded of Mark 3:31–35. There Jesus' mother and brothers send for him, but he says that whoever does God's will is his brother, sister, and mother.

We may say that Jesus creates a new family. Jesus' mother and the Beloved Disciple, who were previously unrelated, are now mother and son. Their relationship with Jesus has led to a new relationship to each other. This reminds me of Mark 10:29: "Truly, I say to you, there is no one who has left house or brothers or sisters or mother or father or children or lands, for my sake and for the gospel, who will not receive a hundredfold now in this time, houses and brothers and sisters and mothers and children and lands . . . and in the age to come eternal life."

It may be that you can relate to the first part of this verse. It may be that since you became a Christian, your relationship with your unbelieving family has been strained, or even broken. There are parts of the world where becoming a Christian puts one at risk of being killed by members of one's own family! It may be that for some other reason your relationship with your family is strained or unhealthy. Maybe you have to keep your distance from them to avoid being affected by their toxicity. My experience on the Prayer Lines tells me that Satan is having a heyday disrupting and perverting family relationships.

My Friend, if this is your situation, know that God has provided a remedy. What Jesus does for his mother and the Beloved Disciple in John 19:25–27, he does for all his disciples to this day. If our relationship with your family of origin is difficult or nonexistent, for whatever reason, let the local church be your spiritual family. Form the healthy relationships with your brothers and sisters in Christ that you could not have with your birth family. It is no accident that in some sections of the church, members call each other "brother" and "sister." This was the practice of the early church (see, e.g., Acts 21:20; Rom 14:10, 15, 21; 1 Cor 5:11; 6:6; 7:12, 15; Heb 13:23; Jas 1:9; 2:15; 4:11). And it is not a coincidence that Paul calls the church "the household of faith" (Gal. 6:10) and "the household of God" (Eph 2:19). Peter tells his readers to "love the brotherhood" (1 Pet 2:17). If you do not have healthy relationships with your earthly family, God is able to replace them with a new, spiritual family.

5. Has someone served as a "spiritual parent" to you? If so, why not express your gratitude to God and to them?

Please read Mark 15:33–37. The first thing that Mark records here is that darkness covered the land for three hours. Some readers, thinking that a solar eclipse is meant, complain that a solar eclipse is astronomically impossible, since Passover is always celebrated at a time of a full moon, and would not last longer than seven minutes, even if it were possible. This is true; but it is beside the point. There can be little doubt that the darkness here is a supernatural darkness, and that it symbolizes God's judgment. Joel 2:2 calls the day of God's judgment "a day of darkness and gloom, a day of clouds and thick darkness!" Amos asks, "Is not the day of the LORD darkness, and not light, and gloom with no brightness in it?" (Amos 5:20). And Zephaniah says, "A day of wrath is that day, a day of distress and anguish, a day of ruin and devastation, a day of clouds and thick darkness" (Zeph 1:15). Especially relevant is Amos 8:9: "'And on that day,' says the Lord GOD, 'I will make the sun go down at noon, and darken the earth in broad daylight'". The mockers have been asking Jesus for a sign—here God gives them a sign, a sign that judgment is beginning. This darkness-judgment is an indication that what is happening is the first round in the end-times battle. Jesus' cry at verse 34 shows that that judgment is falling on him. An old preacher who preached at my church used to say that Jesus was precipitated from the cup of the wrath of man into the bowl of the wrath of God.

Gentile readers of the Gospels would not understand the Old Testament background which we have been discussing. But it was well established in Greco-Roman tradition that extraordinary phenomena occurred when a great man died. For example, according to Roman mythology, when Romulus, co-founder of Rome, died, the sun went dark. And it was said that when Julius Caesar was assassinated, the sun went dark again, and a comet appeared in the sky that night. Gentile readers would understand the darkness to mean that Jesus' shameful death did not make him any less great.

Luke in his Gospel sets up a pattern which joins his Passion narrative to his story of Jesus' birth. Zechariah, celebrating his own son's birth, describes the coming birth of Jesus as a time when "the rising sun will come to us from heaven to shine on those living in darkness and in the shadow of death" (Luke 1:78–79 NIV). In Gethsemane Jesus tells his enemies, "this is your hour, and the power of darkness" (Luke 22:53). That power is at its highest at Calvary.

6. On whom should that judgment have fallen? Why?

That judgment should have fallen on us! It was I and you and every human being ever born who sinned, not Jesus. "For our sake he [God] made him [Jesus] who knew no sin to be sin, so that in him we might become the righteousness of God" (2 Cor 5:21). Of all the people who have ever walked this earth, Jesus alone was sinless. It was not his own sin which was sent him to the cross, but ours. Another story from the making of the *Passion* film illustrates this. It is said that in the shots of the nails being driven into Jesus' hands, the hands holding the hammer are Mel Gibson's own.

Mark next records what is sometimes called the cry of dereliction: "My God, my God, why have you forsaken me?" (Mark 15:33). We must avoid making light of this by saying that Jesus quotes only the first verse of Ps 22 but is thinking of the entire psalm (which ends in triumph and trust), or that Jesus only felt abandoned. As commentator William Lane puts it, "The sharp edge of this word must not be blunted."[4] God's abandonment of Jesus was only temporary, but it was very real (but even so Jesus does not renounce God. He still calls him "my God"). We must remember that sin cuts the sinner off from God. Isa 59:2 says, "your iniquities have made a separation between you and your God, and your sins have hid his face from you." Jesus took our sins upon himself. God then had to turn his back on Jesus, or he would not have been consis-

---

4. *Mark*, 572.

tent. Being separated from God must have been worse for Jesus than the physical suffering inflicted on him by humans. It is what he fears most in Gethsemane, but he endures being forsaken by God so that we could be accepted by God. See what our salvation cost! How can we not be grateful, and awed?

We may ask, "How could God separate himself from Jesus?" Our God is triune, that is, three in one, Father, Son, and Holy Spirit, one God in three Persons. If the Father and the Son are one, how is it possible for the Father to separate himself from the Son? But then, we may just as well ask how the three distinct personalities that make up the Trinity can at the same time be one. Perhaps it is best if we simply accept the fact that these things are, without trying to explain how they can be. There are some things that we will not be able to understand this side of heaven. Meanwhile we can be grateful that Jesus was willing to take our sins on himself, even though it meant being separated from the Father.

Jesus cries out using the words of Ps 22:1. Again we see Jesus connected with David in weakness and vulnerability. Because he cries out in Hebrew, some bystanders misunderstand him and think that he is calling for Elijah, who was believed to rescue those who were in trouble. This also tells against any positive interpretation of the cry of dereliction. The bystanders think that Jesus is calling for help, not that he is expressing trust in God. There is a puzzle here: if the soldiers misunderstand Jesus enough to think that he is saying "Elijah" instead of "My God," how can they be familiar enough with Jewish customs to know about Jewish beliefs about Elijah? It is most likely that they have been in Judea long enough to become familiar with local customs, but have not found it necessary to learn the local language. Many Palestinian Jews spoke Greek as well as Aramaic, so Roman soldiers could communicate with them in Greek.

Someone, probably one of the soldiers, gives Jesus a drink of the soldiers' cheap wine, to keep him alive longer, to see whether Elijah will come and take him down from the cross (ironically, while Elijah will not intervene, God himself soon will). The reader knows that Elijah has already come, in the form of John the Baptist (Mark 9:13). But much of Israel did not recognize him, any more than they have recognized Jesus.

We may also note that the cry of dereliction itself shows that Jesus has not lost faith in God. Only great faith produces such great anguish. If Jesus did not know God was with him, it would not cause him such distress when God turns his back on him. A cynical proverb says, "Blessed are those who expect nothing, for they shall never be disappointed." To expect nothing is a good way to protect ourselves from disappointment. But it is unbelief, not faith. It is to choose to place one's faith in nothing. Faith chooses to put its trust in someone or something, even at the risk of disappointment. Jesus does not give up on God, even in this extreme situation. May we follow his example of never losing faith. May we continue to say, "My God," no matter what our circumstances are.

DAY FOUR

The Lamb of God
Today's key verses: John 19:28–30

Please read John 19:28–30. Jesus says, "I am thirsty." There is an irony here, in that the Jesus who asks a Samaritan woman for a drink, then offers her living water (John 4:7, 10) is thirsty. The emphasis in these verses is on fulfillment. The Greek words in verse 28 translated "finished" and "fulfill" come from the same word, *teleioo;* and the word translated "finished" in verse 30 comes from a related verb, *teleo*. Now, in the New Testament the usual Greek word for the fulfillment of Scripture or prophecy is *pleroo*. John uses *teleo* to emphasize that the fulfillment is now complete.

It would be natural enough for Jesus to be thirsty in the circumstances; but it is also seen as the fulfillment of Scripture. Jesus' thirst fulfils Ps 22:15, "my strength is dried up like a potsherd, and my tongue sticks to the roof of my mouth; you lay me in the dust of death" (NIV). The soldiers' response to his cry fulfils another Scripture, Ps 69:21: "They gave me poison for food, and for my thirst they gave me vinegar". They give him some of their cheap wine (those versions of the Bible that call it vinegar emphasize its poor quality). Jesus symbolically drinks the cup which the Father has given him, as he said that he should (John 18:11). Earlier in the Gospel, John the Baptist has identified Jesus as the Lamb of God (John 1:29, 36). Here at the end of the Gospel Jesus steps into the role prophesied for him. The mention of hyssop also draws attention to Jesus as the Passover Lamb (Exod 12:22).

Having drunk, Jesus cries out, "It is finished!" (John 19:30). This is not a cry of defeat but of victory: *"I've done it! Mission accomplished!"*. Throughout the Gospel of John, Jesus has referred to himself numerous times as having been sent by the Father. He has clearly understood that the Father has given him work to do (John 4:34; 5:36; 17:4). Now Jesus can say that he has accomplished his mission. All the Scriptures surrounding his life and death have been fulfilled, finally and completely. This is the meaning of the Greek word for Jesus' cry, *tetelestai*. It means "to finish; to complete (a mission); to bring (something) to an end; to carry out (someone's) will." The previous evening, Jesus has said, "I have . . . accomplished the work which thou [the Father] gavest me to do" (John 17:4). That work includes laying down his life (John 10:17–18) as the sacrifice prefigured by the Passover lambs.

Perhaps it would be useful to look briefly at the Passover lambs. The story of Passover is narrated in Exod 11:1–12:36. The night that the Israelites left Egypt, God struck down the oldest child, human and animal, in every household in Egypt. But he had told the Israelites how to protect themselves. Each family was to take a lamb and slaughter it, and put some of the blood on the doorframe of their house. "The blood shall be a sign for you, upon the houses where you are," says God. "And when I see the blood, I will pass over you, and no plague shall fall upon you to destroy you, when I smite the land of Egypt" (Exod 12:15). This event is commemorated by Jews to this day, in the holiday of Passover.

How does this apply to us? Jesus is our Passover Lamb. The lambs had to be without blemish (Exod. 12:5); so also Jesus was without sin. Just as the blood of the lambs protected the Israelites from judgment, so the blood of Jesus covers us and protects us from God's judgment. At the cross Jesus took the judgment that should have fallen onto us.

7. How does Paul apply the Passover to our lives in 1 Cor 5:7–8?

Paul applies this to our lives in another way, bringing in the command that during Passover all leaven (that is, yeast) must be removed from the house (Exod 12:19; 13:7; Deut 16:3). Throughout the Bible, leaven is a symbol of sin. This is why it was to be absent at Passover, the celebration of God's redemption and purification of Israel. Likewise, says Paul, Christians must clean the leaven of sin out of their lives. "For Christ, our paschal lamb, has been sacrificed. Let us, therefore, celebrate the festival, not with the old leaven of malice and evil, but with the unleavened bread of sincerity and truth" (1 Cor 5:7–8). Of course we cannot do this on our own (any more than the Israelites could protect themselves from the destroyer that first Passover night), nor does God expect us to. That is why he sacrificed Jesus, our Passover Lamb. It is also why he gives us the Holy Spirit to guide us in living rightly before God. The Spirit warns us about what is wrong in God's eyes, tells us what is right, and helps us to do it (John 14:26; 15:26; 16:13).

8. Turning back to John's use of *teleo*, is there anything missing from what Jesus did at Calvary?

We saw earlier that John uses this word to stress the completeness of Jesus' action. So after Calvary, what is left for us to do for our salvation? We may just as well ask, What *can* we do for our salvation? The answer to both questions is, absolutely nothing! Jesus has done everything that needed to be done so that we could be saved. "We have been made holy through the sacrifice of the body of Jesus Christ once for all" (Heb 10:10). There is nothing that we need to add. No words, no action, no ceremony is needed for our salvation. The death of Jesus is enough to atone for our sin.

In fact we may say that there is nothing that we *can* do to be saved. Nothing that we say or do can cancel out our sin nature and earn our salvation. Our sin puts up a wall between us and God that we cannot climb over or knock down. Sin has taken that ability away from us: "all have sinned and fall short of the glory of God" (Rom 3:23). "I know that nothing good dwells within me, that is, in my flesh. I can will what is right, but I cannot do it" (Rom 7:18). We cannot get out of the prison of sin ourselves. If we could, it would not have been necessary for Jesus to come and die. But Jesus did on our behalf what we could not do for ourselves. What we have to do is to receive by faith what Jesus has done for us. That is all that we can do, and it is all that we need to do.

For some people, that is the problem. Their fleshly pride will not allow them to admit that they cannot help themselves and need God. But this is the first step toward salvation, and it cannot be avoided. This is something that makes Christianity different from all other religions. All other religions say that we can climb up to God if we meditate long and hard enough, do enough good deeds, or follow certain rules carefully enough. Only Christianity says that we could never get up to God, so God came down to us.

DAY FIVE

Into the Father's Hands
Today's key verse: Luke 23:46

Jesus' last word from the cross is, "Father, into thy hands I commit my spirit" (Luke 23:46). The Greek word translated "commit" is *paratithēmi*. It means "to place in someone's care, for safekeeping." It is not used of being put in the hands of one's enemies. This saying is from Ps 31:5. In this Psalm David calls on the Lord in his distress, and expresses confidence that God will deliver him because of his relationship with God. "I trust in thee, O LORD, I say, "Thou art my God . . . .Let thy face shine on thy servant; save me in thy steadfast love! Let me not be put to shame, for I call on thee" (Ps 31:14,16–17).

9. How does this apply to us?

David trusts God to deliver him because of their relationship. Jesus, Son of David, uses the same words to express his trust in God, trust based on his relationship with God (we may note that David, as servant, calls God "Lord," Jesus, as Son, calls God "Father"). So also we who have a relationship with God through Jesus can trust that God will deliver us from trouble because of our relationship with him. We can say, like David in another Psalm, "The LORD redeems the life of his servants; none of those who take refuge in him will be condemned" (Ps 34:22). If God does not take us *out of* our troubles, he will take us *through* them.

Jesus prophesied that he would be delivered into the hands of sinners (Luke 9:44; 24:7). And indeed his opponents have tried to lay their hands on him (Luke 20:19; 22:53). But they are not able to hold him, until the time set by the Father (John 7:6, 30; 8:20). Rather he is in the hands of the Father. He places himself there, which indicates that he is in control.

This word of Jesus brings a sense of completion to his life and ministry. Jesus is conceived by the Holy Spirit (Luke 1:35), and the Spirit descends on him at his baptism (Luke 3:22). He functions in the power of the Spirit (Luke 4:1, 14). So in committing his spirit to the Father, Jesus brings things full circle. His spirit goes back to where it came from.

In all four Gospels the actual notice of Jesus' death is very brief, like the notice of his crucifixion. This is in keeping with the style of the

Gospel writers, who tend to keep to the point as they tell their stories, and avoid extraneous details. The loud cry mentioned by Mark and Matthew is a sign associated with the end times. Ps 46:6 says, "The nations rage, the kingdoms totter; he [God] utters his voice, the earth melts." In Jer 25:30 Jeremiah is told to prophesy, "The LORD will roar from on high, and from his holy habitation utter his voice; he will roar mightily against his fold, and shout, like those who tread grapes, against all the inhabitants of the earth." Joel 3:16 says, "And the LORD roars from Zion, and utters his voice from Jerusalem, and the heavens and the earth shake." In 1 Thess 4:16 Paul tells the Thessalonians that "the Lord himself will descend from heaven with a cry of command, with the archangel's call." And in Rev 10:3 it is an angel who "called out with a loud voice, and like a lion roaring."

None of the Gospel writers uses the usual Greek words for dying to describe Jesus' death. Mark and Luke say that Jesus "breathed his last" (Mark 15:37; Luke 23:46), using the same Greek word, *ekpneo*. This indicates a sudden death; our English word "expire" covers the meaning well. Matthew says that Jesus "let go his spirit" (Matt 27:50), using the Greek word *aphiemi*. John says that Jesus "gave up his spirit" (John 19:30), using the Greek word *paradidomi*. As we have seen in earlier weeks, this is the word used for the actions of Jesus' opponents, as Judas betrays Jesus, the Jewish authorities hand Jesus over to Pilate, and Pilate hands Jesus over to his soldiers for crucifixion. But the last handing over belongs to Jesus, as he hands himself over to the Father. There is a deliberate quality about both *aphiemi* and *paradidomi*; Jesus releases his spirit of his own accord. This is consistent with his earlier claim that no one takes his life from him, but he lays it down of his own accord (John 10:18). Mark's and Luke's use of *ekpneo* does not contradict this.

So far this week, we have discussed Jesus' crucifixion, and what he went through so that we could be saved. But there is also a sense in which we are the ones who must be crucified. Scripture makes it clear that we must crucify the flesh.

We saw in Week 2 that the flesh (not to be confused with the physical body) is the part of human nature that gives in to temptation and sin. Paul says, "those who belong to Christ Jesus have crucified the flesh with its passions and desires" (Gal 5:24). Earlier he has said that the flesh and the Spirit are opposed to each other (Gal 5:17) and that we must choose to be led by either the one or the other. He then lists the results that each produces in our lives: the works of the flesh (Gal 5:19–21) and the fruit of the Spirit (Gal. 5:22–23). I suspect that the reader is supposed to ask, Which of these things do I want operating in my life? Now, if we compare Paul's two lists, that question is a no-brainer! Who really wants to have the works of the flesh—strife, jealousy, anger and the rest—when they can have love, joy, peace, and the other fruit of the Spirit? But if we want to escape from being controlled by the flesh (which is our natural state) we must kill it. If we do not kill the flesh, it will kill us.

We have seen this week that crucifixion was an extremely painful and humiliating death. Perhaps that is why Paul says that the flesh must be crucified, instead of saying that it must be put to death by the sword or by a dose of hemlock. Those would be quicker deaths than crucifixion. Under the guidance of the Spirit, Paul is acknowledging that killing the flesh is not easy, because the flesh does not die quietly. Putting our flesh to death is often a struggle. It involves humbling ourselves—before God, and sometimes before other people as well. It involves discipline, saying No to ourselves even when it is uncomfortable. It is a battle we can win, with the help of the Holy Spirit and the prayers and support of our brothers and sisters in Christ.

10. If the flesh is a problem for you, why not ask someone in the group to pray with you?

Throughout his ministry Jesus has been battling evil, in the form of healing the sick and casting out demons. The only word from the cross which Mark records is the cry of dereliction; his readers might get the impression that Jesus has lost the battle. He is dead, abandoned (apparently) by God. They might wonder if he can offer them help or hope in their own struggle against enemies who were persecuting them for being his disciples. But the story is not over yet.

WEEK 6

Sealed in a Stone-Cold Tomb

DAY ONE

No Bone Broken
Key verses: John 19:31–42; Mark 15:38–41;
Matt 27:51–53, 62–66

LAST WEEK WE STUDIED Jesus' actual crucifixion and death. This week we will turn our attention to some things that happened after his death, and to his burial. We will see events through the eyes of various people who see what happens. Please read John 19:31–37. It is Friday afternoon, the Sabbath is approaching. And it is no ordinary Sabbath, it is the Sabbath of Passover Week. So "the Jews" ask Pilate to order his soldiers to break the crucified men's legs, which would hasten their deaths. With broken legs they could not push themselves up on the crosses to ease their breathing. This would allow that their bodies be taken down from the crosses and buried before sunset, and the land would not be defiled (see Deut. 21:22–23). There is an irony here that is similar to the irony at John 18:28: "the Jews" are scrupulous about avoiding ceremonial defilement, but have executed an innocent man. The soldiers break the legs of the other men, but when they come to Jesus they do not break his legs, because he is already dead. To confirm this, a soldier stabs him in the side with a spear, which produces a flow of blood and water from Jesus' side.

Much symbolism has been attached to this scene. But it is best to interpret it according to the indications which John has given us. In one sense, the flow of blood and water prove that Jesus came in the flesh, and that his death was real, not imaginary. There has been much speculation as to exactly where the blood and water come from, and several doctors have written about the physiological cause of Jesus' death (perhaps this is the point to remember what we saw on Day Five of last week: Jesus releases his spirit, and his life, of his own accord). But John's interest is theological, not medical. He is writing a Gospel, not a medical textbook or an episode of *CSI: Crime Scene Investigation*! So why does he want to stress that Jesus really died? Some time around AD 100 there emerged the heresy of Gnosticism, which said (among other things) that Jesus was not actually flesh but a phantom, or that it was not Jesus who was crucified but a phantom, or that the soldiers believed that they were crucifying Jesus but actually crucified Simon of Cyrene. The problem seems to have been that the Gnostics could not understand how Jesus could be fully human as well as fully divine. After some two thousand years of church history, we can easily miss how hard to understand this concept is, especially those of us who were raised in church. Apparently Gnostic ideas had already begun to emerge when John wrote his Gospel, which was around AD 80. This is why he insists that the Word became flesh (John 1:14). And later, in a letter, he will say that anyone who does not confess that Jesus came in the flesh is a deceiver (2 John 7). This may also explain why he insists that he saw the piercing and the flow of blood and water for himself (John 19:35).

1. Why is it important to us today that Jesus really died?

Gnosticism has long since faded into obscurity. So is it important to us today that Jesus really died? Yes, for two reasons. First, a death is still required to atone for sin. "Without the shedding of blood there is no forgiveness of sins" (Heb 9:22). Jesus could not be our Savior if he had only pretended to lay down his life. The blood sacrifice had to be real in order for it to be effective. A pretend sacrifice does not atone for our sins. Second, there is the question of the accuracy of Scripture. Jesus predicts his own suffering and death, not a substitute's (Mark 8:31; 9:12; 10:33–34; John 3:14; 8:28; 12:34). And the death that he predicts is real, not an illusion. It is as important today as it ever was that we know that the written Word of God can be trusted.

Is there no symbolic meaning to the flow of blood and water? We must be careful not to exercise our imaginations to the point where they take us beyond what the text actually allows. We may safely say that the flow of blood symbolizes the life-giving nature of Jesus' death. "Truly, truly, I say to you, unless you eat the flesh of the Son of man and drink his blood, you have no life in you; he who . . . drinks my blood has eternal life . . . For . . . my blood is drink indeed" (John 6:53–55). Jesus gives his life for the life of the world (John 6:51). We saw last week that just as the blood of the Passover lambs protected the Israelites from death, so the blood of Jesus protects us from God's deadly judgment on our sin. Death is the wage that we earn for sin, but what God gives us in Jesus is eternal life (Rom 6:23). This is another sense in which the death of Jesus gives us life.

The flow of water looks back to John 7:37–39, where Jesus promises that from his insides will flow rivers of living water. John then explains that this refers to the Spirit, not yet given. The outflow of water from Jesus' side is a foretaste of Pentecost. We will study Pentecost in Week 8. Here I will say only that the giving of the Spirit at Pentecost is made possible by Jesus' death at Calvary. We may also mention that in John 4:10 Jesus offers the Samaritan woman living water. She asks him where he will get this water, since he has nothing to draw water with (John 4:11). Here her question is answered. The water comes from Jesus' own side, and he gives it not only to the Samaritan woman but to anyone who believes (John 7:37).

It is significant that John mentions the flow of blood before the water. Why this order? We can answer this question by considering the symbolism which we just discussed. The blood represents the fact that Jesus died to give us life, and the water represents the Holy Spirit. They come in this order because we must have this life—a crucified life—before we can have the benefits that come with being filled with the Holy Spirit. We will consider this further in Week 8.

John says that what the soldiers do, and what they refrain from doing, fulfils Scripture. The Scripture referred to in verse 36 is probably either Exod. 12:46, "you shall not break a bone of it [the Passover lamb]," or Num. 9:12, "They shall leave none of it [the lamb] until the morning, nor break a bone of it." In this way John again draws attention to Jesus as the Passover Lamb. The Scripture quoted at verse 37 is Zech. 12:10. In the original Hebrew the part of the verse which John quotes reads, "they will look upon me, upon the one whom they have pierced," and God is the speaker. In the original context the meaning is that Israel will realize that they have pierced (i.e., grieved) God by their sins, and will mourn. Here John may be saying that one day those who rejected Jesus will realize their sin in doing so, and will repent (this would tell against the idea that John's Gospel is anti-Semitic). It is also interesting that Zech 12:10 refers to mourning for an only son (in John 1:18; 3:16, Jesus is called God's only Son). So in its original context this verse refers to God the Father, but in its application in John's Gospel it refers to God the Son.

2. What is John's purpose in writing, according to John 19:35?

The middle of this verse, where John insists that his testimony is true, is a parenthetical note. The rest of this verse reads, "He who saw it has borne witness, that you also may believe." He saw the piercing and the flow of blood and water, and this is what he testifies to. He wants the reader to believe that these things happened, and that they happened in accordance with Scripture (see verses 36–37). Verse 35 is connected to verses 36–37 by "for." John is saying, in effect, *I saw these things, and I am telling you so that you can believe, because these things happened in order to fulfill Scripture, so it is right for you to believe.* We saw in Week 1 how important it was to the church to show that Jesus' death fulfilled Scripture. We also saw earlier today that John was concerned to fight Gnostic ideas by showing that Jesus really died. Those who believe that Jesus came in the flesh and that his death brings us life, all in fulfillment of Scripture, will receive the Holy Spirit, which is symbolized by the flow of water from Jesus' side.

DAY TWO

The Veil is Torn
Today's key verses: Mark 15:38–41

Yesterday we saw how, in fulfillment of Scripture, Jesus' legs were not broken, and his side was punctured with a spear. John testifies to what the saw, and the fact that he saw it is clearly important to him. But he is not the only one watching what happens. In today's passage, another event leads someone else to testify. Please read Mark 15:38–41. At Jesus' death the veil of the temple is torn in two, from top to bottom. The passive "was torn," and that the tearing goes from top to bottom, show that it is God who is doing the tearing. Mark uses the same Greek word for "was torn" here as the one that the RSV translates "were opened" in Mark

1:10. There the heavens are torn open as God puts his stamp of approval on Jesus, at the beginning of his ministry: "Thou art my beloved Son." Here as the veil is torn the centurion confesses Jesus as Son of God.

The veil referred to is probably the inner veil, a thick curtain which separated the Most Holy Place, or Holy of Holies, from the rest of the temple. The Most Holy Place was, above all other places on earth, the place where God was present. Access to that place was limited: only the high priest was allowed to enter there, and that only once a year. And he did not dare to come in without an offering of blood, which atoned for his sins and the people's. But the death of Jesus has changed all that. The tearing of the veil indicates that access to God is no longer limited. Since Jesus offered the perfect sacrifice—himself—anyone who accepts that sacrifice for themselves by faith has access to God. And we must note that it was God himself who opened way for us to have access to God. We could not do it for ourselves. Only God could tear the veil.

Under the law, sin was atoned for by the blood of sacrificial animals. But animals could provide only a temporary forgiveness for sins. That is why it was necessary to offer the sacrifices regularly, over and over again. They were only a type, a symbol, of what was to come. They pointed to what was really needed. What was needed was a sacrifice which exceeded the animals as only a human can. That is why Jesus, the perfect man, offered himself. Once he had done this, there was no need for animal sacrifices. "[Jesus] entered once for all into the Holy Place, taking not the blood of goats and calves but his own blood, thus securing an eternal redemption. For if the sprinkling of defiled persons with the blood of goats and bulls . . . sanctifies for the purification of the flesh, how much more shall the blood of Christ, who through the eternal Spirit offered himself without blemish to God, purify your conscience" (Heb 9:12–14). "The blood of Jesus [God's] Son cleanses us from all sin" (1 John 1:7).

3. What does it mean to you that the veil has been torn?

Now that God has torn the veil, that means that anyone who believes has direct access to him. Because of our relationship with Jesus, we have direct access to the throne room of heaven. We can come before God with our needs and our weaknesses. We do not need to be afraid or ashamed, because Jesus our High Priest understands what it is like to be human. "For we have not a high priest who is unable to sympathize with our weaknesses, but one who in every respect has been tempted as we are, yet without sin. Let us then with confidence draw near to the throne of grace, that we may receive mercy and find grace to help in time of need" (Heb 4:15–16). We do not have to clean ourselves up before we come to God. The truth is that we cannot clean ourselves up. But if we have a relationship with Jesus, God sees us through the filter of Jesus. God looks at us and sees not our sin but Jesus' perfection.

The tearing of the veil also shows that the temple building no longer serves its purpose; it is no longer a holy place. Jesus has cleared it of those who have turned it from a house of prayer into a den of robbers (Mark 11:15–17), and prophesied that it will be destroyed (Mark 13:2). Jesus' opponents have accused him of threatening to destroy the Temple (Mark 14:58; 15:29). Ironically, it is they who will bring about the Temple's destruction, at the hands of the Romans.

When the centurion in charge of the execution squad sees how Jesus dies, the sight leads him to make a confession. "Truly this man was the Son of God," he says (you may remember John Wayne's hilariously bad delivery of this line in the film *The Greatest Story Ever Told*). But what does he mean by this? By "truly" the reader is to understand that he rejects any false ideas about what it means to be Son of God. Only those who see that Jesus completes his mission by dying can rightly understand what it means to say that Jesus is Son of God. The path to glory leads through suffering. Jesus' opponents have been unable or unwilling to see this, and so have not recognized Jesus for who he is. The idea that the Messiah would suffer was a major stumbling block in the way of Jews coming to believe in Jesus.

It is interesting that the centurion says, "Son of God," not "King of the Jews." His statement ignores the political issue raised in the Roman trial and turns the reader's attention back to the issue raised before the Sanhedrin. As with the Pilate trial, the issue of politics is subordinate to another issue. Here the issue that is in the forefront is Jesus as the suffering Son of God.

The last time that the phrase "this man" appeared in the Gospel of Mark was when Peter said, "I do not know this man you are talking about" (Mark 14:71). The contrast between the two statements is clear. Peter denies Jesus, the centurion confesses him. We may also note that both are at risk. Peter is at risk of being arrested like his Master, and the centurion may find himself in trouble with his superiors if he is heard saying something that is favorable to a man being executed as a revolutionary. The centurion shows the courage which Peter cannot yet muster.

Mark begins his Gospel with a statement of what the book is about: "The beginning of the good news of Jesus Christ, the Son of God" (Mark 1:1). And in Mark 1:11 God tells Jesus, "You are my beloved Son." The demons recognize Jesus as Son of God, which is why he often silences them (Mark 1:34; 3:11-12). Humans, however, have not been so quick to recognize Jesus. Peter says that Jesus is the Christ (Mark 8:29), but the rest of the story makes it clear that he does not fully understand what it means for Jesus to be the Christ. Here at the cross a human finally makes the same evaluation of Jesus as God. And the irony is that the human who does so is not a disciple, nor even a Jew, but a Gentile soldier. Earlier Jesus said, "I, when I am lifted up from the earth, will draw all men to myself" (John 12:32). He referring to his crucifixion, as John explains (verse 33). Even as he dies his prophecy begins to be fulfilled. This centurion is the first of many Gentiles to believe, as Jesus begins to draw all people to himself.

The Romans, however, are not the only ones watching what happens. Some women who have accompanied Jesus during his ministry are watching from a distance.

4. How do these women disciples compare with Peter (for a hint, see Mark 14:54)?

As Peter follows from a distance in Mark 14:54, these women watch from a distance. Later they will try to anoint Jesus' body, just as Peter tries to follow Jesus on his own; neither will succeed. The women may be more faithful than the male disciples (most of whom are in hiding), but they too have their failings as disciples. But they do not give up on God or on themselves, and they stay close to God and to each other.

This is encouraging for us. Like them, we all have our failings as disciples of Jesus. None of us gets it right all the time. We must not think that those first disciples were any different from us. They had the same ups and downs in their walk of faith as we do. Like them, we need to stay close to God and to each other, and not be embarrassed to be honest with one another. We are all tempted to "put our church face on" and make it look as if we have it all together. The truth is that we all have our problems, and acting as if they are not there will not make them go away. It is better to be honest about our problems and get the help we need.

I am not suggesting that we should tell the world about our problems. But it is a good idea to share our needs with one or two people whose wisdom and spiritual maturity we can trust, so that they can pray with us and for us, and keep us accountable. I have heard it said that God did not intend us to be "Lone Ranger Christians," but members of the Body of Christ, under the spiritual authority of the church. Many times, when I encourage people to find a vibrant, Bible-believing church, they will say, "I have to clean myself up before I can go to church." But this is doing things in the wrong order. If we have gotten off-track, we need the support of the church to get back on track.

Another thing that we may say about these women is that they "ministered to him [Jesus]". The Greek word is *diakoneo*, which means, "to serve; take care of." This means that they did the traditional "women's work" for Jesus and the Twelve. Yes, they washed Jesus' clothes! They cooked his meals! How is this significant for us? We cannot cook Jesus' meals, but we can cook meals for Jesus. We cannot wash his clothes, but we can wash clothes for Jesus. In other words, we serve him when we do these things for others. If you are a stay-at-home mother, do not underestimate the value of the "mundane" things you do every day. They are the tasks that God has called you to, and you please him when you do them diligently and well, as if you were doing them for him.

DAY THREE

Earthquake!
Today's key verses: Matt 27:51–53

Please read Matt 27:51–53. Matthew says in his account of Calvary that some other supernatural phenomena accompany Jesus' death: there is an earthquake which breaks rocks and opens tombs. Many "holy ones" are raised from the dead, and in succeeding days appear to many. In other words, there are signs in the heavens (the darkness), signs on earth (the earthquake, the rocks, the tombs), and signs under the earth (the risen dead). They are all signs that in a sense the end times have begun with Jesus' death. The centurion and his men see the earthquake and the split rocks, and many inhabitants of Jerusalem see the risen dead.

The earthquake signifies God's wrath. 2 Sam 22:8 says, "Then the earth reeled and rocked; the foundations of the heavens trembled and quaked, because he [God] was angry." Here David, celebrating how God has delivered him from Saul and his other enemies (2 Sam. 22:1), mentions God's protective anger against anyone who hurts those whom God loves. This is relevant to our context in Matthew as God reacts to Jesus' death. Isa 24:19–20 says, "The earth is utterly broken, the earth is rent asunder, the earth is violently shaken. The earth staggers like a drunken man, it sways like a hut; its transgression lies heavy upon it, and it falls, it will not rise again." Nahum 1:5 says of God's judgment on Nineveh, "The mountains quake before him, the hills melt; the earth is laid waste before him, the world and all that dwell therein." Rev 6:12 describes what happens when the sixth seal on the scroll of God is opened: "behold, there was a great earthquake; and the sun became black as sackcloth…" Here two of the supernatural phenomena associated with Calvary are joined again, one last time. Jer 4:23–24 mentions darkness, an earthquake and the moving of the hills: "I looked on the earth, and it was void; and to the heavens, and they had no light. I looked on the mountains, and lo, they were quaking, and all the hills moved to and fro." In Mark 13:8 Jesus lists earthquakes among the signs of the beginning of the end times.

5. What immediate effect does the earthquake have (see Matt 27:54)?

We have seen that the earthquake signifies God's wrath and judgment on sin, and draws attention to the last-days aspects of what is happening. But it also has an immediate effect: the centurion and his men are afraid, and recognize Jesus as son of God (Mark focuses on the centurion, but that does not contradict Matthew's including the other soldiers). Fear (that is, reverential awe) is the proper response when humans see God intervening in earthly affairs; these Gentile soldiers are able to discern that God is acting to show his approval of Jesus. They are quicker to understand who Jesus is than the Jews who are nearby. In this is the soldiers are like the magi of Matt 2:1–12, and Pilate's wife (Matt 27:19). This pattern is Matthew's way of reproving the Jewish leadership for being slow to recognize Jesus, when they should have been the first to do so.

As for the split rocks, the reader might remember Zech 14:4–5, which describes God's coming in judgment: "On that day his feet shall stand on the Mount of Olives which lies before Jerusalem on the east;

and the Mount of Olives shall be split in two from east to west by a very wide valley; so that one half of the Mount shall withdraw northward, and the other half southward. And the valley of my mountains shall be stopped up, for the valley of the mountains shall touch the side of it; and you shall flee as you fled from the earthquake in the days of Uzziah king of Judah. Then the LORD your God will come, and all the holy ones with him." Isa 26:19 refers to the raising of the dead in the final judgment. And Dan 12:2 says, "And many of those who sleep in the dust of the earth shall awake, some to everlasting life, and some to shame and everlasting contempt." Jesus seems to have the verse in Daniel in mind in John 5:28–29, "the hour is coming when all who are in the tombs will hear his [the Son of man's] voice and come forth, those who have done good, to the resurrection of life, and those who have done evil, to the resurrection of judgment."

The risen saints of Matt 27:52–53 are surely godly Jews. The tombs are opened by the earthquake which immediately follows Jesus' death. Jesus' death breaks the power of death. So after his resurrection these godly Jews follow him in resurrection, and appear to many in Jerusalem. They probably have glorified bodies (unlike Lazarus of John 11:1–44) and probably go to heaven at Jesus' ascension. This would illustrate that Jesus is the first fruits of the dead.

6. If Jesus is the first fruits of the dead, what hope does that provide for us?

The first fruits was an offering that consisted of the first part of each crop to be harvested (Exod 23:16, 19). This first part of the crop was a sort of down payment from God, a guarantee that there would be more to come. When Jesus rose from the dead, that was God's guarantee to us that more people would follow Jesus in resurrection. Paul explains: "But in fact Christ has been raised from the dead, the first fruits of those who have fallen asleep. For as by a man came death, by a man has come also the resurrection of the dead. For as in Adam all die, so also in Christ shall all be made alive. But each in his own order: Christ the first fruits, then at his coming those who belong to Christ" (1 Cor 15:20–23). "He [Christ] is the head of the body, the church; he is the beginning, the first-born from the dead, that in everything he might be pre-eminent" (Col 1:18). Paul also uses this truth to comfort second-generation believers who are distressed by the death of other believers: "For since we believe that Jesus died and rose again, even so, through Jesus, God will bring with him those who have fallen asleep. For this we declare to you by the word of the Lord, that we who are alive, who are left until the coming of the Lord, shall not precede those who have fallen asleep. For the Lord himself will descend from heaven with a cry of command, with the archangel's call, and with the sound of the trumpet of God. And the dead in Christ will rise first; then we who are alive, who are left, shall be caught up together with them to meet the Lord in the air; and so we shall always be with the Lord." (1Thess 4:14–17).

This includes us! Because Jesus rose from the dead, some day we will rise also. This is the hope of heaven! Remembering this allows us to look at what happens in this life from an eternal perspective. Most of what happens in this life does not seem as big and bad when we view it from the perspective of eternity. Things that seem to have little importance in this life take on a different meaning when we look at them with eternity in mind. The reverse is also true; from an eternal perspective, things that seem important in this life may not seem so important. It also means that we can take comfort in knowing that one day we will be reunited with loved ones who died in the Lord.

It is also interesting that the first fruits offering was to be of the highest quality. The Hebrew word *reshith* means first in quality as well as in time, and that is its meaning in Exod 34:26. The NIV translates correctly: "Bring the best of the firstfruits of your soil to the house of the LORD your God." Since Jesus is without sin, he qualifies in this area as well. Peter says that Jesus "committed no sin; no guile was found on his lips" (1 Pet 2:22). He also says that we have been redeemed "with the precious blood of Christ, like that of a lamb without blemish or spot" (1 Pet 1:19). Similarly Heb 9:14 says that Jesus "offered himself without blemish to God." And again, "By his [God's] will we have been sanctified through the offering of the body of Jesus Christ once for all" (Heb 10:10). And Paul describes Jesus as "a fragrant offering and sacrifice to God" (Eph 5:2). So he is entirely qualified to be the first fruits of the dead.

We may also note that Matthew says that these risen saints go into "the holy city" (Matt 27:53). The only other time that he has used this phrase is in Matt 4:5, where the devil takes Jesus to the holy city and challenges him to prove that he is the Son of God by jumping of the roof of the temple, to see if God will send an angel to catch him. But Jesus will not play the devil's games. During the temptation, he refuses to prove that he is God's Son. The raising and appearances of these saints is the proof that was demanded in the temptation. And it is not Jesus who supplies the proof, but God himself (the passive "were raised" indicates that it is God who does the raising).

DAY FOUR

A New Tomb
Today's key verses: Mark 15:42–47

So far this week we have seen the events surrounding Jesus' death through the eyes of several witnesses: the Beloved Disciple, the centurion and soldiers who crucify Jesus, and the people of Jerusalem. Another person who sees what happens is Joseph of Arimathea, a godly and respected member of the Sanhedrin. Please read Mark 15:42–47. Joseph goes to Pilate and asks that Jesus' body be released to him for burial. This takes courage, because a Roman governor would not normally release the body of a man executed for treason; he would be likely to think that anyone who asked him to do so was a sympathizer, even an accomplice, of the executed man. Pilate is surprised to hear that Jesus is already dead, and sends for the centurion to inquire. We saw last week that crucifixion was a lengthy death, which is why Pilate is surprised. Not that this is the first time that Jesus has surprised someone. In Mark 1:22, 27 the people of Capernaum are amazed as Jesus teaches and casts out a demon. In Mark 5:20 the people of the Decapolis are amazed at the testimony of the (formerly) demon-possessed man of Gerasa. Here Jesus still has the power to amaze, even in death.

When the centurion confirms that Jesus is dead, Pilate releases Jesus' body. Mark uses the word "corpse" in verse 45 to stress the reality of Jesus' death. That Pilate releases the body is a sign that he believes that Jesus was innocent. Throughout most of the Roman Empire, the corpses of the crucified were left on their crosses to rot. But in Judea, as a concession to the Jewish law, they were usually buried quickly in a common grave.

Joseph buys a linen cloth for a shroud, and has the body carried to a nearby tomb, hewn out of the rock, closing it with a large stone. The tomb is a newly-made one (Matt 27:60; Luke 23:53; John 19:41),

Matthew adding the detail that the tomb is Joseph's own. This makes sense, in view of the haste that is needed because the Sabbath is coming. There is no time to make a new tomb, but Joseph knows where there is an available tomb to which he has access. The reader gets the impression of a hasty burial, as Joseph does what he can in the time he has.

7. After reading what happens in Mark 6:29, what might the reader expect to happen here?

In Mark 6:29, John the Baptist's disciples take their master's body from Herod's prison for burial. This is risky, because the tetrarch who has just executed the master is likely to do the same to his disciples. Having read what John's disciples do, the reader is likely to expect Jesus' disciples to do the same for him. Instead it is Joseph who takes courage and goes to Pilate and asks for Jesus' body. The Eleven, who should perform this duty, are in hiding.

A word about Jewish burial customs in the first century is in order at this point. Burial took place on the day of death. The deceased was carried to the tomb on a bier, accompanied by a procession of relatives, friends and professional mourners. The body was washed, then anointed with fragrant oils. It was wrapped in a shroud, or strips of cloth, of wool or linen. Spices were also sprinkled into the shroud as the body was wrapped. This was done to counteract the odor of decomposition, since the Jews did not embalm the dead (one year after burial, the bones would be placed in a rectangular stone ossuary). The jaw was tied closed, and the head wrapped in its own cloth. The arms were placed along the sides of the body, and the ankles tied together, before the body was wrapped. The pottery containers used for the spices and ointments were considered unclean, so they were left in the tomb.

The tomb would have been dug out of the rock, a short, small (about 16" x 24"/40 x 60 cm.)[1] entrance tunnel expanding first into an antechamber, then into a chamber high enough to stand up in, about 2m/6.5' square. In some tombs, horizontal cavities (*arcosolia*), in which the bodies would be laid, were cut into the walls of this room. In others, small (about 16 x 16"/40 x 40 cm.) tunnels some 7'/2.5 m. long, called in Aramaic *kokhim*, in Latin *loculi*, were dug into the walls, and the bodies placed in head first. Both *arcosolia* and *loculi* were about 3'/1m. above the floor of this inner chamber. The entrance would be closed with a large

---

1. For all these measurements I am following Gibson, *Final Days*, 155–56.

stone, to keep unpleasant odors in and tomb robbers out. These tombs were usually family tombs. Most first-century tombs were closed with a square or rectangular stone, or a boulder. But the Evangelists clearly describe a stone that could be rolled (Mark 15:46; 16:3, 4; Matt 27:60; 28:2; Luke 24:2), so it must have been disk-shaped. A few tombs closed by disk-shaped stones have been found. Interestingly, these tombs are all from Jesus' time. By the time the Gospels were written, disk-shaped stones were no longer in use. This is a point in favor of the accuracy of the Gospel record.

When we consider this, we can see that Jesus receives a typical burial. We may assume that Joseph of Arimathea washes the body when it is taken down from the cross. Otherwise the women would bring water to the tomb along with the spices (Mark 16:1). No Jew, even one who had died a criminal's death, would have been denied this basic rite. Once Jesus is laid in the tomb, there is no time to do anything else for him until after the Sabbath. But then the women come with spices to finish what they have begun. The women see a young man sitting on the right side (i.e. the right side of the slot where Jesus' body had lain, Mark 16:5), and Mary Magdalene, when she returns to the tomb a second time, sees two angels "sitting where the body of Jesus had lain, one at the head and one at the feet" (John 19:12). This implies that the tomb of Jesus was an *arcosolium* tomb.

Where was the tomb located? The Gospel writers are not specific about this. But John says that it was near the execution site (John 19:41), which makes sense in view of the haste needed. The Church of the Holy Sepulcher marks the place identified by tradition as both Calvary and the burial site; there is no archaeological or literary reason to believe that the tradition is incorrect. It is within the boundaries of present-day Jerusalem, but outside the walls of Jerusalem in Jesus' time. Unfortunately, the building of memorials to what happened there that first Easter weekend has, over the centuries, obscured what that place would have looked like when those events occurred.

Mark notes briefly that two women, both named Mary, see where Jesus is buried; we will see the significance of this later. For now we will say only that the church is unlikely to have made this up, because in the first century women were not considered valid witnesses.

We turn now to a story found only in the Gospel of John; please read John 19:38–42. John says that Joseph is joined in burying Jesus by Nicodemus, a Pharisee and a leading member of the Sanhedrin, who brings a quantity of spices. They seem to work as a team: while Joseph goes to Pilate, Nicodemus goes to the market to buy what is needed before the market closes for the Sabbath.

Nicodemus appears only in the Gospel of John, but this is the third time that he appears in that Gospel. In John 19:39 John refers to Nicodemus' first appearance in the Gospel (John 3:1–21), so he wants us to remember that passage as we interpret this one. In John 3:1–21, Nicodemus comes to Jesus at night. This is more than just a time indication. Nicodemus is also in the dark spiritually, as he is unable to understand what Jesus says about spiritual birth. Jesus clearly expects him to understand: "Are you a teacher of Israel, and yet you do not understand this?" (John 3:10) he asks. As a member of the Sanhedrin, it is his job to investigate reports of miracles. He sees Jesus as "a teacher come from God" (that is, a prophet; John 3:2), but nothing more.

Nicodemus reappears in John 7:50–52. Here he reminds the Sanhedrin that they cannot convict Jesus without a hearing. This seems like a step forward. But his faith is tentative at best. He is not standing up for Jesus so much as for proper procedure. After Jesus dies he is finally ready to take a public stand for Jesus. We may also note the amount of spices that Nicodemus brings. John 19:39 says that he brings "about a hundred pounds' weight." This would be one hundred Roman pounds, about 75 modern pounds, or 34.5 kg. If Mary of Bethany (she is not to be confused with Mary Magdalene) anoints Jesus with one pound of oil of nard, worth 300 *denarii* (John 12:1–8)—a year's wages for a laborer—Nicodemus brings a hundred times that much. This is a large amount, enough for a royal burial. If the Roman soldiers mock Jesus as King, Nicodemus buries him as King.

8. What is interesting about the timing of Joseph's (and Nicodemus') coming forward?

At the same time as the Eleven go into hiding, two disciples who have not been heard of before come forward. I do not believe that this timing is a coincidence. God always has someone to speak up for him. In 1 Kings 19:18, Elijah thinks that he is the only Israelite left who has not abandoned

God. But in fact God has "seven thousand in Israel, all the knees that have not bowed to Baal, and every mouth that has not kissed him."

We may also say that the appearance of these two wealthy men at this time allows for the fulfillment of the first part of the prophecy of Isa 53:9: "They made his grave with the wicked, and with a rich man in his death."

Joseph and Nicodemus are men of wealth and status who are likely to lose their position in society if they identify themselves with Jesus. So perhaps it is understandable that it takes them a while to gather enough courage to step forward. After all, Jesus warns would-be disciples to be aware beforehand of the cost of discipleship (Luke 14:25–33). It seems that the wealthy Joseph (and the equally wealthy, if not wealthier, Nicodemus) have decided that the eternal rewards of being a disciple of Jesus are worth whatever cost they may have to pay in this world. In this they are to be contrasted with Pilate, who, as we saw in Week 4, condemns Jesus to the cross rather than risk Caesar's wrath. They are also to be contrasted with the rich young man who asks Jesus what he must do to inherit eternal life, but is unwilling to give up his possessions to get it (Mark 10:17–22).

Joseph and Nicodemus are "closet Christians." But being a "closet Christian" is not enough. Disciples of Jesus must be public about their discipleship. This does not mean that we should be rude or obnoxious about letting people know that we are Christians. But neither should we be ashamed. Indeed Jesus warned, "If anyone is ashamed of me and my words in this adulterous and sinful generation, the Son of man will be ashamed of him when he comes in his Father's glory with the holy angels" (Mark 8:38). This is not something that I, for one, want! God forbid that I should give him cause to be ashamed of me! If we do not want him to be ashamed of us then, we must not be ashamed of him now. May we, like Nicodemus and Joseph, be faithful servants who will take a stand for our Master.

DAY FIVE

A Stone, a Seal, a Squad of Soldiers
Today's key verses: Matt 27:62–66

Please read Matt 27:62–66. It is "after the day of Preparation," that is, it is the Sabbath. But ironically, the Jewish authorities are not honoring the Sabbath. They go to Pilate again, this time to ask him to place a guard of Roman soldiers at Jesus' tomb. They call him, in Greek, *kyrios*, which can be translated either "sir" or "Lord." This title has been reserved for Jesus up to this point. The effect is similar to their saying, "We have no king but Caesar" (John 19:15).

The Jewish authorities are concerned that Jesus' disciples might steal his body and make it look as if he has been raised from the dead. For them, this would be a greater deception than Jesus (whom they call "that impostor") predicting his resurrection in the first place (Mark 8:31; 9:9; 10:34). This is the only place in the Gospels where the Jewish authorities call Jesus an impostor. But the related verb is used in John 7:12, 47, where it is a question of whether or not Jesus is leading the people astray.

Ironically, these opponents of Jesus take what he said more seriously than his disciples do. The disciples do not understand what Jesus meant when he predicted his resurrection (Mark 9:10). The Jewish authorities assume that the disciples will try to make it look as if Jesus has returned from the dead. All that any human can do to produce an empty tomb is to steal the body. God, on the other hand, is able to empty the tomb by raising the body. It is also ironic that the Jewish authorities anticipate that the disciples will act deceitfully, but they are the ones who will act deceitfully (Matt 28:13–15). Perhaps the biggest irony of all is that from the first Easter until today, the disciples' preaching of the resurrection has brought more people to Jesus than his earthly ministry, which was necessarily limited in time and space, did. If the Jewish authorities of that day could see this, they would certainly say that the last fraud (as they saw it) is worse than the first!

There has been some question as to whether Pilate says at verse 39, "Take a guard," that is, "You may take a squad of my men," or "You have a guard," that is, "You have your own men, temple attendants; use them."

In fact, we know that Pilate says, "Take a guard," for two reasons. First, the word translated "soldiers" in Matt. 28:12 is *stratiotai*, which usually refers to Roman soldiers. Second, if the guards were Jewish temple attendants, they would not need to be concerned about Pilate's possible reaction to their sleeping while on duty (Matt 28:14). So the guards at the tomb are Roman soldiers, probably another squad of four.

The Jewish authorities take these soldiers and seal the tomb, leaving the guards there. But their precautions will not be enough to stop God's plan of salvation from being carried out, any more than Herod can stop it at Jesus' birth (Matt 2:16). The seal would consist of two disks of beeswax, each stamped with Pilate's seal (or the seal of the Sanhedrin). One of these would be pressed onto the stone, the other onto the façade of the tomb, near the stone. The wax disks were connected by a piece of twine, one end pressed into each disk. Such a seal was not so much a physical barrier so much as it was backed by the power and authority of the person doing the sealing. A modern example would be yellow police tape blocking off the scene of an incident. POLICE LINE DO NOT CROSS. The real barrier is the knowledge that anyone who crosses the line without authorization is likely to be arrested. The seal is to keep the guards honest: if someone bribes them to allow the tomb to be unsealed and the body stolen, the seal will be damaged and the soldiers will be unable to claim that nothing happened. As to the question of historicity, we may say that if Matthew had made this story up himself, he would probably have had the guards posted immediately after Jesus' burial instead of after an interval during which the body could have been stolen.

9. How does Paul apply Jesus' death to us (for a hint, see Rom 6:1–14)?

Paul applies Jesus' death to us in an unexpected way. Because Jesus died, we as his disciples are dead to sin. Sin has no power over us! This is both an encouragement and a challenge to us. We who have asked Jesus to come into our lives are joined with him in his death. Paul says, "The death he died he died to sin, once for all, but the life he lives he lives to God. So you also must consider yourselves dead to sin and alive to God in Christ Jesus. Let not sin therefore reign in your mortal bodies, to make you obey their passions" (Rom. 6:10–12). We do not have to give in to sin. We can be as unresponsive to sin as a corpse is when someone talks to it. We sometimes say of someone who is so soundly asleep that they do not hear anything that is happening around them that they are "dead to the world." Just so, we can be so dead to sin that we do not hear it when it calls us. "We were buried with [Jesus] by baptism into death, so that as Christ was raised from the dead by the glory of the Father, we too might walk in newness of life" (Rom 6:4). This does not mean that once we are born again we will never sin again. It is a fact that until we get to heaven there will be times when we stumble. When this happens we must run to God for cleansing, receive his forgiveness, and get back on track. We can be assured that God will welcome us back. John says, "If we say we have no sin, we deceive ourselves, and the truth is not in us. If we confess our sins, he [God] is faithful and just, and will forgive our sins and cleanse us from all unrighteousness...My little children, I am writing this to you so that you may not sin. But if any one does sin, we have an advocate with the Father, Jesus Christ the righteous; and he is the expiation for our sins, and not for ours only but for the sins of the whole world" (1 John 1:8–9, 2:1–2). In fact Paul is not talking in Romans 6 about occasional stumbles. He is talking about a pattern of repeated sin. This is something that should not be happening in the life of a born-again, Spirit-filled Christian. "How can we who died to sin still live in it?" (Rom 6:2) Paul asks. If you find yourself falling into the same sin over and over again, even though you genuinely want to stop, you need to find out why this is happening. There is some root problem that has not been dealt with. But there is help. As a born-again, Spirit-filled Christian, you have the Holy Spirit living inside you. He will help you break free. Ask God to show you what the problem is. You may want to set aside a time for prayer and fasting, and to speak with a professional counselor.

As Christians, we are dead to sin. It is not our master any more. We do not need to let it control us any longer. We can live the way God wants us to. We can have the victorious life God wants us to have. We can be free to serve him, which is to be truly free. That is what it means to walk in newness of life.

> **10. Do you have a testimony about how God has set you free from a pattern of repeated sin that you could not get free of yourself? If it is appropriate, why not share with the group?**

That Friday night, Jesus was dead and buried, the entrance to the tomb blocked by a stone, a seal and a squad of soldiers. Was heaven itself holding its breath, waiting to see what would happen next?

WEEK 7

A Happy Beginning

DAY ONE

The Stone Rolled Away
Key verses: Mark 16:1–8; Luke 24:9–12; John 20:3–18

THE PHRASE WHICH I have used as the title for this lesson comes from New Testament scholar N.T. Wright, who said that the resurrection of Jesus is not a happy ending to the story of his earthly ministry, but a happy beginning to the new creation which has been inaugurated by the death and resurrection of Jesus.[1] "According to his promise we wait for new heavens and a new earth in which righteousness dwells" (2 Pet 3:13). This new creation will not be fully manifested until the end (Rev 21:1). But it began with the death and resurrection of Jesus, which is also what makes it possible. And we see hints of it even now, in the restored lives of those whom Jesus has healed and delivered.

It is interesting that the New Testament Gospels do not describe the resurrection itself. "None of the New Testament writers dares to describe Jesus' emergence from the tomb . . . The mystery must not be trivialized by idle words. This awed restraint reminds us that the resurrection is not a carefully constructed myth but an inexplicable event. The story is credible only because God is credible."[2] The evidence is

---

1. "The Resurrection of Jesus Christ—Part 1" *Haven Today* radio program originally broadcast March 24, 2008. Accessible at www.haventoday.org./bishop-nt-wright-resurrection-jesus-christ.p.1594.html.
2. Hare, *Matthew*, 331.

set out, and the reader, like the characters in the Gospel stories, must decide to believe or not.

From its beginnings the church was aware that the resurrection was central to its faith (see e.g. Acts 2:24, 32; 3:15, 26). And Paul tells the Corinthians, "if Christ has not been raised, your faith is futile" (1 Cor 15:17, compare verse 14). He also says, "I delivered to you as *of first importance* what I also received, that Christ . . . was raised on the third day in accordance with the Scriptures," 1 Cor 15:3, emphasis added). From earliest times Christians spoke of Jesus' *resurrection* or his *being raised*. To Jews (which these earliest Christians were), these words could only mean coming out of the grave. This means that the empty-tomb stories are an important part of the resurrection story. As one scholar puts it, "Apart from the discovery of the empty tomb, the Easter appearances of Jesus would in all probability be interpreted as ghost stories, in effect turning Easter into Halloween."[3] It is no surprise, then, that the story of the empty tomb is found in all the Gospels. A major factor in favor of the historicity of the empty-tomb story is that the first people to see that the tomb is empty are women—not something which the church would invent, since it is embarrassing to the male disciples. Besides, in ancient Jewish and Roman society, women were not considered valid witnesses. If the church had invented this story, it would have had men discover the empty tomb. We may also note that the resurrection was first preached within weeks of its occurrence, in the city where it happened. Such preaching would hardly have been successful if the tomb had not been empty, because if the church's opponents had been able to show that the tomb was not empty, they would have done so.

As in the last two weeks, we must combine the Gospels to get the whole picture, because each Evangelist, under the leading of the Holy Spirit, tells the parts of the story that best suits his purpose. So how do we combine the pieces into a coherent whole? Especially, how do we combine John's account with those of the Synoptic Gospels? I suggest that a combined account might look like this:

1) A group of women go to the tomb at sunrise (Mark 16:1–3; Matt 28:1; Luke 24:1–3; John 20:1). John focuses on Mary Magdalene, but she says "we" in John 20:30, so a group of women is in view.

2) An angelic visitation—the women are sent to tell the disciples that Jesus has risen (Mark 16:4–8; Matt 28:2–8).

---

3. Evans, *Mark*, 2:531.

3) The women go to the men, most of whom do not believe the women's report (Luke 24:9–12; John 20:2). 3) Peter runs to the tomb (accompanied, in the Gospel of John, by the Beloved Disciple) to see what has happened. Peter sees the empty tomb and the grave clothes, but does not understand and leaves wondering (Luke 24:12; John 20:3–7), but the Beloved Disciple sees and believes (John 20:8–9).

4) Mary has followed them back to the tomb; she is so discouraged by the others' doubt that she only returns to faith when Jesus himself appears to her (John 20:11–18).

Please read Mk. 16:1-8. Two of the women who witnessed Jesus' death and burial —Mary Magdalene and another Mary—buy aromatic oils with which to anoint Jesus' body and complete the customary burial rites. They are accompanied by Salome, who saw Jesus' death but not his burial (it appears that they have bought the oils on Saturday evening, after the Sabbath, to use on the Sunday). Clearly they are not expecting the resurrection. Who holds a funeral for someone whom they believe will rise from the dead? But we must not be too hard on these women. After all, none of the men was expecting it either—and understandably so. After all, in the realm of normal human experience, the dead do not come back to life. So it is not surprising that they are not expecting Jesus to return from the dead. He told them that he would, but they did not understand what he meant.

The women wonder who will roll the stone (which probably weighed 1½–2 tons) away from the tomb entrance—but when they arrive they find the stone already rolled away. Entering the tomb, they see a young man in white, sitting on the right side, the side of power and favor. It is clear that he is an angel. He tells them not to be afraid, which is usually the first thing an angel says when meeting a human (compare e.g. Dan 10:12; Luke 1:13, 30; 2:10). He announces to them that Jesus has risen and gives them a message for the disciples, including Peter: they are to go to Galilee, where they will meet Jesus, as he had told them earlier (Mark 14:28). "Just as he told you" (verse 7) is a reminder of how many of Jesus' prophecies have been fulfilled. The women leave in haste, silence, and fear. Their fear is comparable to the disciples' fear as Jesus calms the storm (Mark 4:41) and heads toward his fate in Jerusalem (Mark 10:32), and the Gerasenes' fear when Jesus delivers the man possessed by a legion of demons (Mark 5:15). It is the usual human response to God's intervention in earthly affairs.

> **1. Throughout the Gospel of Mark Jesus has commanded his disciples, and others, to be silent (Mark 1:44; 3:12; 5:43; 8:30; 9:9); here the command is to speak. Why?**

The command is to speak, because now there is no possibility of misunderstanding what kind of Messiah Jesus is. Here is no glorious military Messiah come to set up a political Kingdom of God on earth. Here is a suffering and dying Messiah who has sacrificed himself for sin. The time for silence is over—now is the time for proclamation! We may also note that while the command to be silent is usually disobeyed, this command to speak is apparently obeyed. The women must have eventually told someone. If they had not, no one else would have known what happened. There would have been no preaching of the resurrection, no church and no New Testament!

Critics have said that the story of the women coming to the tomb, which is found in all three Synoptic Gospels (that is, the Gospels of Matthew, Mark, and Luke), is inconsistent with the story of Nicodemus bringing spices to the tomb, which is found only in the Gospel of John. Why would the women bring spices if Nicodemus has already done so? One possible explanation lies in non-communication. Since Nicodemus is a closet disciple, the women may not know about his plan to bring spices. But they see where Jesus is buried. Is it likely that they watch where Joseph lays Jesus, and leave before Nicodemus arrives? It is also possible that the women see that Nicodemus has brought powdered spices, but not the oils which were also customary. It is more likely that it is a matter of everyone doing what they can. Mary of Bethany anoints Jesus in preparation for his burial; "She has done what she could," he says (Mark 14:8). The wealthy Nicodemus brings 30,000 *denarii* worth of myrrh and aloes. Mary Magdalene and the other women are not as wealthy as Nicodemus, but they can afford to bring oils.

There is a lesson for us here, and it may have nothing to do with money. Each of us has a contribution to make, and we should do what we can. We may not be wealthy, but we can be generous with what we have, and we can contribute in ways that are not financial. Someone who is not physically strong can still be a mighty prayer warrior; someone who cannot get out of the house can encourage both themselves and others by talking to other shut-ins on the telephone. Someone who owns a car can offer rides to those who do not. No contribution is too small if it is made in order to serve God by serving others.

For me, the story of the women at the tomb is mainly about "finding God in the dark." From the point of view of these women, Jesus is dead and buried. He has done great deeds, so much so that his disciples have put their faith in him as one who has God's stamp of approval. Suddenly he is dead, in the most humiliating way possible, indeed in a way that seems to place him under God's curse (Deut 21:23; Gal 3:13). Now an angel has told them that he has risen from the dead, and will meet them in Galilee, keeping a promise he made (Mark 14:28)—but he himself is nowhere to be seen. It looks as if he has let them down. Now they must choose whether to rely on what they can see or on Jesus' word. Perhaps they remember that most of the prophecies Jesus made while he was alive have come about. Can they trust him for this one? Will they? In another sense, the reader is supposed to ask, "What will I do when the circumstances are difficult and God seems to be absent?" Those are the times when a disciple of Jesus must choose to trust him in spite of the circumstances, which is not always an easy thing to do.

2. Do you have a story to share about a situation in which you had to choose to trust God? If it is appropriate, why not share it with the group?

DAY TWO

To Emmaus and Back

Today's key verses: Matt 28:11-15; Luke 24:9-49; John 20:3-18

Please read Luke 24:9-12; John 20:3-18. When the women tell the male disciples that Jesus has risen, the men do not believe them; what they say seems like a foolish story. But Peter goes to the tomb to see for himself. Does he think, or hope, that there is something in the women's report? Does he think that if what the women say is true, there might be some way to redeem himself after his stumble? Does he think that grave robbers may have struck?

According to the Gospel of John, Peter is accompanied to the tomb by the Beloved Disciple. There has been much discussion among the scholars of what it means that the Beloved Disciple beats Peter to the tomb. The best explanation is probably the traditional one, that the Beloved Disciple is younger than Peter. This may also explain why the Beloved Disciple defers to Peter by allowing Peter to enter the tomb first.

When they enter the tomb, the see the grave clothes, but no body. This proves that grave robbers have not struck, because grave robbers would hardly take a naked corpse and leave the valuable cloth and even more valuable spices. Peter is confused, but the Beloved Disciple "saw and believed" (John 20:8). What does he believe? It appears that he believes that Jesus has risen, on the basis of the abandoned grave clothes rather than on the basis of the Scriptures, because none of the disciples yet understands that the Scriptures point to the resurrection. The Beloved Disciple is the only disciple to believe on the basis of the empty tomb. The others do not believe until they see the resurrected Jesus for themselves.

The mention of the tomb and the grave clothes reminds the reader of the raising of Lazarus (John 11:1–44). But while Lazarus needs help to get out of his grave clothes, Jesus does not. Perhaps this is because Lazarus is raised to more physical life, and will die again, but Jesus is raised to spiritual life, and will not die again (compare Rom 6:9, "Christ being raised from the dead will never die again; death no longer has dominion over him").

Meanwhile, Mary has returned to the tomb; she is standing outside the entrance, weeping. Looking into the tomb, she sees two angels, who ask her why she is weeping. She expresses her despair: "They have taken away my Lord, and I do not know where they have laid him" (John 20:13). Her emotions, perhaps encouraged by the men's doubts (Luke 24:11), are threatening to overwhelm her faith. In the midst of this, Jesus appears to her. What changes is not Mary's circumstances, but her attitude toward them. Jesus is still not physically present. But Mary's unbelieving despair becomes proclaiming faith when she realizes that he is still with her.

Mary does not recognize Jesus until he calls her by name. Jesus the Good Shepherd calls his sheep by name, and they know his voice (John 10:3–4). There has been much discussion of what his instruction, "Do not hold me," means. The most likely meaning is, "Do not cling to me." Mary needs to understand that she cannot have the same relationship with the risen Jesus as she had with Jesus in the flesh. But that does not mean that her relationship with him is over. The risen Jesus will be with her, just no longer in visible form. He will be with her in the form of the Holy Spirit (John 14:26; 16:7; 17:23).

Jesus gives Mary a message for the disciples: "I am ascending to my Father and your Father, to my God and your God." What does this mean? The disciples are children of God just as Jesus is Son of God. Because they have believed in him, Jesus has given them the right to be God's children (John 1:12). The sonships are different, because while Jesus is Son by birth (John 1:14; 3:16), the disciples are sons and daughters by adoption (Rom 8:23; Eph 1:5). But the similarities are emphasized more than the differences.

Please read Matt 28:11–15. While the women are going to the disciples to tell them what has happened, the guards go into Jerusalem to report to the Jewish authorities that Jesus' body is missing. Their announcement contrasts with the women's announcement to the disciples that Jesus is risen. The guards and the women see the same thing, but they respond differently. There is a lesson for us here. The women are able to see what God is doing because their hearts and minds are tuned to him. Like a radio picking up a particular station, we can tune our hearts and minds to hear from God. We cannot do this on our own, but the Holy Spirit acts as our tuner, helping us to pick up what God is broadcasting. We also do our part by regularly spending time in prayer, Bible study, and church attendance. We must make sure that our hearts and minds are open like these women's, and not closed like the hearts of the soldiers.

The Jewish authorities take counsel (verse 12). They have taken counsel against Jesus before, looking for a way to put him to death (Matt 26:3–4; Mark 3:6; 11:18; John 11:45–53). Now they take counsel to look for a way to cover up the fact that he is not dead any more. Like the guards, their minds are closed. What they hear might be enough to change their minds, if their minds were not already firmly made up (I am sure that we all know people like that!) They decide to bribe the guards to say that they fell asleep and Jesus' disciples stole the body. They reassure the guards that they will keep the guards out of trouble with Pilate—a serious concern, because Roman soldiers caught sleeping on duty would be court-martialed and, if found guilty, executed (this is the concern in Acts 16:27–28). But the soldiers are willing to take the money, just as Judas was. The false story which they tell is still circulating among the Jews, Matthew says, as he writes his Gospel.

Please read Luke 24:13–49. Later that same day, two disciples, one named Cleopas and the other unnamed, are walking to a village called Emmaus, not far from Jerusalem. The exact location of Emmaus is uncertain. This goes in favor of the historicity of this narrative, because it is unlikely that a resurrection appearance would be connected to an obscure location unless it actually occurred there.

The disciples are discussing what has happened in the previous few days. The words used indicate that the conversation is an intense one, and no surprise—it is not as if they have nothing important to discuss! As they are talking, Jesus himself joins them, but they do not recognize him. Ironically, they are getting what they hope for, but they do not know it. The passive "were held" indicates that God is keeping them from recognizing Jesus. Some scholars think that Satan is blinding their eyes, but he is not mentioned in this context. The two disciples are shocked to find that this stranger has apparently not heard about the events that so occupy their own minds. The disciples think that this stranger does not know about recent events, but in fact he knows more about what has happened than anyone! The reader is aware of this, so this is an opportunity for the reader to have some amusement at the expense of the disciples.

Since the stranger seems to be uninformed, Cleopas explains who Jesus was, what happened to him, what his disciples were expecting from Him, and the women's news of that morning. One may say that in verses 20–21 Cleopas considers the evidence that they were mistaken about Jesus (Jesus was condemned by the Jewish authorities and executed), and in verses 22–24 he considers the evidence that Jesus is the Messiah (the women's report, partially confirmed by the men). The reader is also supposed to weigh the evidence and decide whether Jesus is the Messiah.

It appears, however, that more is needed than just the bare evidence. Before anyone can come to saving faith, the Scriptures must be explained to them, and they must have enlightenment that can come only from the Holy Spirit. This is what Jesus provides for these two disciples. It is the same in all evangelism. We are responsible for sharing our faith and the Scriptures with non-believers. But to give a non-believer understanding of the Scriptures and bring them to faith is the job of the Holy Spirit. And if we do our part, he will do his.

By this time they have reached the village. The two disciples, thinking that their new acquaintance intends to go on further, encourage him to stay the night with them, because it is getting late. Hospitality was an important part of ancient Mediterranean society, and traveling at night was dangerous. The three share a meal, and Jesus acts as host. This meal is not a re-enactment of the Last Supper, or of the Feeding of the Five Thousand. But Jesus' actions with the bread (taking, blessing, and breaking) are the same. Luke surely intends that the reader be reminded of these events, and of their own communion service.

3. Why would Luke, as he tells his story, connect these events?

The same Jesus who fed the five thousand, and who hosted the disciples at the Last Supper, now hosts two disciples at a post-resurrection meal. This is how he shows them that he is still with them, even if not in physical form, and that he will continue to meet their needs. This is a repeated theme in the stories of the resurrection appearances. We, who are used to Jesus being spiritually present with us, may not understand how startling this would have been to those who had had him physically present with them. But once they understood this, we can be sure that they took great comfort in Jesus' continuing presence. We also can take comfort in knowing that the same Jesus whom we read about in the Gospels is present with us in our need. He is also the same Jesus whom Luke's original readers, and disciples to this day, commemorate as we take the bread and wine.

It is at this point that the disciples recognize Jesus, even as he vanishes from sight. If in verse 16 "their eyes were held," in verse 31 "their eyes were opened." They seem to feel that they should have recognized him earlier, when their hearts burned within them as he talked. Immediately they rush back to Jerusalem, to tell the other disciples what has happened. But the other disciples have their own news: "The Lord has risen indeed, and has appeared to Simon!" (Luke 24:34).

Just then Jesus appears among them. At first they are alarmed, thinking that they are seeing a ghost. But Jesus shows them his wrists and feet (which presumably have nail marks) to identify himself, and eats a piece of fish to prove that while he may have a glorified body, he is not a ghost. He rebukes them for their lack of perception, because they should recognize him.

Verses 44–46 look back, as Jesus explains his words and the Scriptures (note how the two are linked) to the disciples. Verse 49 looks forward, as he tells them how to prepare for what is coming next. Before they can preach, they must be empowered. The disciples can testify because they are witnesses (verse 48). They have experienced:

- The preaching and teaching of Jesus during his lifetime
- The Passion events which fulfilled Scripture
- The fact of the resurrection
- The risen Jesus' opening of the Scriptures to them

4. What does this tell us about our own witnessing (for a hint, see Mark 5:18–20)?

In Mark 5:18–20 a Gentile man whom Jesus has freed from demon possession asks to go with him. But Jesus has a better plan. "Go home to your friends," he says, "and tell them how much the Lord has done for you, and how he has had mercy on you" (Mark 5:19). We can draw two things from this. First, our witnessing starts at home. If we cannot witness to our own family and our own community, we will not be able to witness to people of another culture in a distant land. Of course, witnessing this close to home presents its own challenges. Those closest to us are the ones who will see best whether we "walk the talk," and whether our faith is making a difference in our own lives. If we cannot deal with these at-home issues, we will not be able minister effectively elsewhere.

Second, our strongest testimony is about what God has done for us, and how he has made a difference in our own lives. This will speak more clearly to others than purely theological conversation (and the good news is, telling others what God has done for us requires no Bible-school training). "He put a new song in my mouth, a song of praise to our God. Many will see and fear, and will put their trust in the LORD" (Ps 40:3; compare Pss 35:17–18; 71:22–23; 118:17–18; 142:17).

At this point I should say a word to those who do not have the kind of history that sounds so good at testimony meetings. There are those who have fallen into a pit of sin and God has brought them out of it, for their good and his glory. But what about the rest of us? I was a "nice girl" growing up; I never got involved in "sex'n'drugs'n'rock'n'roll," or any of the other things that teenagers can fall into. I will say two things to people like me. First, we must not think that we need God, and the salvation he offers, any less than the most depraved of sinners. "All have sinned and fall short of the glory of God" (Rom 3:23). "If we say we have no sin, we deceive ourselves, and the truth is not in us" (1 John 1:8).

Second, we can testify to what God has protected us from. The stories told by people who have been deep in sin sound amazing, but those people usually bear the scars of the sin they have come out of. Third, we "nice girls" must remember that "there but for the grace of God go we." If God has kept us from falling, or jumping, into a pit of sin, he has done so only by his grace and mercy, not because we have deserved it. Our attitude should be one of humble gratitude. Above all we should avoid proud self-righteousness, which is as offensive to God as the most sinful action.

DAY THREE

Seeing and Believing
Today's key verses: John 20:24–31; Matt 28:16–20

Please read John 20:24–31. It is a week after the resurrection. One of the Twelve, Thomas, was not with the disciples when Jesus appeared to them. Now they have gathered together again, and this time Thomas is with them when Jesus appears again. Thomas has been skeptical about the resurrection: "Unless I see in his hands the print of the nails, and place my finger in the mark of the nails, and place my hands in his side, I will not believe" (John 20:25). Perhaps Thomas does not want to be hurt again. Jesus' death was a crushing blow to Thomas; to believe that Jesus has risen from the dead and then find out that he has not would be a greater disappointment than Thomas could bear. Better not to believe without proof. And maybe Thomas does not want to give his allegiance to anyone who is not Jesus. So he wants proof that this man who is claiming to be Jesus really is Jesus.

Jesus takes up the challenge. He appears and invites Thomas to touch as he said he wants to (which shows that Jesus hears his disciples even when he is not physically present). But Thomas does not need to touch—seeing Jesus is all the proof he needs. "My Lord and my God" (John 20:28) is the last and highest confession in this Gospel. It is a confession which can be made with understanding only after the resurrection. To make this confession is to honor the Son as one honors the Father (John 5:23). Jesus calls down blessings on those who have believed in him without having the kind of absolute proof which the disciples have had. "Blessed (i.e., accepted and approved by God) are those who have not seen, but have believed anyway" (John 20:29).

This verse sums up the theme of signs-faith which runs through the Gospel of John. In John 2:23–25, we read that many people have believed in Jesus because they have seen him do miracles. But Jesus does not entrust himself to them, because he knows human nature. In other words, he puts no confidence in them, because he knows that faith based solely on miracles is not strong enough to withstand testing. In John 4:48 Jesus tells a royal official that people will not believe in him unless they see signs and wonders (the Greek word for "you" is plural). He wants to find out whether the official's faith is placed in miracles or in Jesus who does the miracles; the man passes the test, and the boy is healed. Here Jesus says that while Thomas believes because he has seen, there is an extra blessing for those who believe even though they have not seen.

"Therefore" of verse 30 connects verses 30–31 to what precedes: *"Those who believe without seeing have God's approval, therefore this book is written so that you might believe, even though you have not seen."*

5. What do these verses tell us about the importance of testimony?

The connection between these verses is important, because those who believe through the disciples' preaching (John 17:20) will not have the opportunity to believe because they have seen Jesus in the flesh for themselves. They can only believe through what they hear from those who did see. This is why John says, "the life was made manifest, and we saw it, and testify to it, and proclaim to you the eternal life which was with the Father and was made manifest to us—that which we have seen and heard we proclaim also to you" (1 John 1:2–3). This is still true today. Those who have never known God can only know him through our testimony of what we have experienced with God.

Why does Jesus invite Thomas to touch him, when he has told Mary not to (John 20:17)? The answer lies in their different needs. Mary needs to understand that her relationship with Jesus will be different from now on. Thomas needs to understand that the Risen One is the same Jesus whom he knew in the flesh. Mary needs to avoid touching Jesus' resurrection body, but Thomas needs to touch that body to identify Jesus (but let us note that having seen Jesus, Thomas no longer needs to touch).

Please read Matt 28:16–20. Jesus has directed the disciples to a mountain in Galilee, and there they go. They all worship him, but some doubt. The Greek word for "doubted" in verse 17 is *distadzo*. It does not refer to unbelief or perplexity—there are better words which Matthew could have used if these were what he meant. Rather it refers to hesitation and indecision. "It is natural to believe that the eleven disciples would have been in a state of hesitation and indecision. Too much had happened too fast for them to be able to assimilate it. They did not doubt that it was Jesus whom they saw and whom they gladly worshipped."[4] This fits in with an important theme in the Gospel of Matthew, that of the disciples having little faith (Matt 8:26; 14:31; 16:8; 17:20). In spite of their emotions, Jesus commissions them to continue what he has begun, and assures them of his continuing presence and support.

All authority in heaven and on earth has been given to Jesus. By his obedience to God, Jesus has obtained far more than he would have if he had bowed down to Satan (Matt 4:8–9). That would have been taking the easy way out. That is what the temptation (Matt 4:1–11) is about. Satan is trying to persuade Jesus to try to accomplish his mission by some other, easier way than the cross. We must be careful not to assume a direct connection between difficulty and evil. When hard times come, we tend to think that they are caused by Satan. But sometimes God brings hard things into our lives to strengthen and train us for his service. Other times God allows the enemy to cause difficulties in our lives. This can only happen when God allows it (Job 1:2; 2:6; Luke 22:31). When he does allow it, we can be sure that God will use what the enemy does, for our good and God's glory. As Joseph says to his brothers, "You meant evil against me; but God meant it for good" (Gen 50:20).

Jesus has been exalted through death and resurrection, so he has been given all authority. Therefore he can commission his disciples to go and make disciples of all nations. Jesus' mission begins again, in Galilee where it began, the disciples replacing Jesus, by his empowerment. But the mission is now on a new level. Jesus confined his own mission to Galilee, Judea, Samaria and Transjordan, but his disciples will go to all nations.

---

4. Hagner, *Matthew*, 885.

The disciples are to teach others to keep Jesus' commands. The same word is used for keeping the law of Moses (Matt 19:17; 23:3). Disciples of Jesus are to obey his teachings just as they have obeyed the law as set down in the Scriptures (remember that these first believers were Jews). In verse 15 the soldiers do "as they were directed." The Greek word translated "directed" is better translated "taught." The Jewish authorities teach the soldiers to tell a lie, but in verse 20 Jesus tells the disciples to teach all nations to observe what he has commanded them. The difference between the two groups is clear.

In the Greek of verse 19, the idea of going is subordinate to the idea of evangelization and teaching. The best translation is, "As you go along, make disciples . . . and teach." This suggests to me that Jesus' commission to evangelize and teach should be part of our daily lives, something that we do all the time. There are those whom God has specially gifted to evangelize or to teach (1 Cor 12:28; Eph 4:11). But we can all share our faith with those around us, and encourage our brothers and sisters in Christ to grow spiritually. We may also say that our assignment from Jesus is twofold. We are to make disciples, but we are not to stop there. Once people have become Jesus' disciples, we must teach them to obey Jesus' commands. This is the ongoing process of encouraging disciples to grow to spiritual maturity.

Matthew ends his Gospel with Jesus' promise, "I am with you always, to the close of the world" (Matt 28:20). "I am with you" reminds the reader of the prophecy at the beginning of this Gospel: "'his name shall be called Emmanuel' (which means, God with us)" (Matt 1:23). Jesus takes for himself the name which is prophesied for him at his birth, the name prophesied for him by Isaiah (Isa 7:14). The Greek phrase translated "always" in Matt 28:20 is *pasas tas hemeras*, literally "all the days." This phrase emphasizes that fact that Jesus is with his disciples every day. Thus Matthew ends his Gospel by looking back to Israel's past (the reference to Isaiah), to the present commission to the disciples, and to the future ("the close of the world"). Jesus is the factor that connects all three.

5. What does it mean to you that Jesus says, "I am with you always"?

This promise is for us just as much as it was for those first disciples. Our Immanuel is with us—he is with *you*! His presence with us is something that we can rely on, not because of our worthiness but because of his promise. We may also note that his promise is to be with us "all the days," not just on the good days. Nor is he with us only on the days when we can feel his presence. His presence is a promise, not just a feeling. He is with us always. My Friend, if you are going through a difficult time, know that Jesus is with you. Choose to believe what he has said, even if your circumstances seem to say something else. I know that that is not easy. But he will not abandon you or let you down. If he does not take you out of your trial, he will take you through it, and you must allow him to decide which one he does, and when he does it. Trust him to keep his promise.

DAY FOUR

The Ones That Did Not Get Away
Today's key verses: John 21:1–23

Please read John 21:1–23. Verses 1–14 could be called the most unusual "fish story" ever. Most "fish stories" are about "the one that got away;" this one is about 153 that did not get away! Several of the disciples are gathered by the Sea of Galilee, including Peter, the Beloved Disciple, and the sons of Zebedee. They decide to go fishing. This does not mean that they have given up being disciples. After all, "the disciples must still *eat!*," as one scholar points out.[5] That being the case, it is natural that they would fish to obtain food, since some of those present are fishermen. We may also say that they are waiting for a "go-ahead" from Jesus, and it is better for them to be occupied than to be doing nothing. Their efforts, however, are unsuccessful. Early in the morning Jesus stands on the beach, but the disciples do not recognize him (are their eyes held, like the eyes of the two disciples on the road to Emmaus?). If they cannot see him, he can see them. He asks them how successful they have been: *"Boys, you do not have any fish, do you?"* In the Greek, the phrasing of the question expects the answer No—Jesus is well aware that they have none. He knows that they are helpless on their own (John 15:4–5; never in the Gospels do the disciples catch fish without Jesus' help). He tells them to throw their net on the right side of the boat, and their obedience is rewarded with a huge catch. The miracle allows the Beloved Disciple to recognize him. It is in character that the Beloved Disciple should be the first of all the disciples to recognize Jesus, and Peter the first to act.

---

5. Beasley-Murray, *John*, 399.

Jesus is preparing a meal of bread and fish for them, and tells them to bring some of their fish. So Peter drags the net ashore. Is he trying to earn his way back into Jesus' good books? But earning one's way into God's good books is unnecessary, and impossible. It is unnecessary because God's grace is not about what we do for him, it is about his unconditional love for us; it is impossible because grace is given, not earned. The disciples contribute to the meal which Jesus provides. If his contribution comes first, they have their part to play too.

7. What does this tell us about discipleship?

We may learn three things about discipleship from this. First, as in Luke 24:30, the risen Jesus still serves his disciples. While this may seem obvious to us, those first disciples would need to learn it. Second, apart from Jesus they can do nothing (John 15:5). They cannot do what he has called them to do without his presence and help.

Third, he calls the disciples to join in what he has begun. They must have his help, but Jesus calls his disciples, then and now, to join with him in what he is doing in the world. It is often said that God calls his people to be his hands and feet in the world. He does not do this because of our abilities, as if he needs our help, but by his grace and because he has chosen to work that way.

There are 153 fish in the net. The number is such an unusual one that many have exercised their imaginations to find significance in it. Several suggestions have been made, all involving various types of number symbolism. But such symbolism requires rabbinical training, and a written copy of the Gospel to study. As interesting as these theories are, the simplest solution is the best: John says that there are 153 fish because there are in fact 153 fish. The fishermen-disciples would count them as they are sorting them in preparation for taking them to market (which is what one would expect fishermen to do with a catch of fish). Or maybe they count them because it is such an amazingly big catch that they want to find out exactly how many fish there are!

After the meal, Peter has an encounter with Jesus that is personal, but not private. As Peter has boasted publicly and failed publicly, so he must be restored publicly. The time of day and the charcoal fire (verse 9, compare John 18:18) connect this story to that of the denials. Jesus asks him, "Do you love me more than these other disciples do?" The issue is whether he will continue his boasting after his failure. Peter makes no excuses, just throws himself on Jesus' love and mercy. Before God can use Peter, Peter must face his faults and acknowledge his need of Jesus. But once he does, he is far better in ministry than if he had never stumbled.

This passage tells us some important things about repentance. The first step in true repentance is acknowledgement of our sin and our need of God's help. If we justify ourselves, or make excuses ("I know what I did was wrong, but…"), we have not really repented. But we can be assured that if we genuinely repent and ask God to forgive us, he will forgive. "If we confess our sins, he is faithful and just, and will forgive our sins and cleanse us from all unrighteousness" (1 John 1:9). Then we need to receive God's forgiveness and move on. Otherwise the enemy may use our past sin as an opportunity to drag us down and keep us from functioning effectively for God, long after God has forgiven us. Once sin is forgiven, it is time to leave it in the past. Ps 51 is a model prayer for forgiveness. David acknowledges his sin and his need for God (verses 1–6), asks God for forgiveness and cleansing (verses 7–12), and promises to tell others what God has done for him (verses 13–17).

Peter's threefold confession of love for Jesus balances his threefold denial of Jesus. It calls forth a threefold commission of Peter as chief undershepherd. He has acted like the hired hand (John 10:12), but he will do so no longer. His past has been confronted and healed, so now he can leave it in the past. That being done, he can accept his present commission and his future destiny. Indeed Jesus predicts that Peter will glorify God by his death (John 21:19)—he will give his life for the sheep as Jesus did (John 10:11). "Stretch out your hands" (John 21:18) is an expression used in other first-century literature to refer to crucifixion. According to church tradition, Peter died by crucifixion in the persecution of AD 64.

All this suggests that God set up the circumstances of Peter's denial of Jesus. If it was Satan who led Peter to deny Jesus, then we may say that God used Satan's attack on Peter for Peter's good, God's glory, and the furtherance of God's plan for the salvation of the world. Why would God arrange, or allow, such an event? It is part of his plan to use Peter. Peter's arrogant self-reliance and pride are fatal attitudes to any minister. God shows Peter his faults, in no uncertain terms. Peter learns (the hard way!) that he must rely on God or he will fail. God can only use Peter if Peter understands this. And once Peter learns about his own faults, he will be more understanding and compassionate in dealing with the faults of the people whom he is to minister to.

In John 21:19 Jesus tells Peter, "Follow me." Following Jesus is an important word in this Gospel for discipleship. In John 13:36 Jesus tells Peter that he cannot follow him now into glory, but will follow him later. It is interesting that there is no Greek word for "following" in its noun form. Following in the New Testament is always a verb—it is an action. In the New Testament, Jesus is the only one who is followed.

In a physical sense, Jesus' call to Peter to follow him is an invitation to a walk on the beach. When Peter sees the Beloved Disciple following them, he asks Jesus what will happen to the Beloved Disciple. Jesus' reply in verse 22 means, "His relationship with me is between me and him. You concentrate on following me yourself."

8. What does this tell us about comparing ourselves with others?

Comparing ourselves with others is not helpful, in fact it can be counterproductive. It is interesting how our standard of comparison changes with our mood. If we are in a good mood, we will probably compare ourselves with those who are not doing as well as we are (and make ourselves feel even better). If we are in a bad mood, we are more likely to compare ourselves with those who are doing better than we are, and end up feeling worse about ourselves than we already do. This is hardly objective!

Besides, we must remember that God works in the lives of believers as individuals. We must not limit him by expecting him to make us cookie-cutter copies of each other. Finally we must be aware that we usually do not know all the facts about our brothers and sisters in Christ. But God does. So if there are issues in another believer's life, we must let God deal with them, as and when they are ready.

A rumor has spread through the church that the Beloved Disciple will never die, but he himself debunks this rumor through careful attention to what Jesus actually said. Jesus did not say, "I want him to stay alive until I come," but "*If* I want…" We also must pay close attention to what Scripture says as we study it, learning to handle the Word of truth correctly (2 Tim 2:15). This is the only way to avoid wrong ideas and false doctrine which can hurt us and others.

The story of Jesus' resurrection is the story of the greatest reversal in history. As one scholar puts it, "God has seemingly thrown a cruel curve at his people…[but] the curve ball has not been thrown to humankind but to sin, death and Satan."[6] For the disciples, it looks as if all their

---

6. Bock, *Luke*, 3:1923.

hopes are dashed. But on seeing the risen Jesus they realize that all their hopes have been fulfilled, though not in the way that they expected. But they are not to keep this good news to themselves: the announcement of the resurrection is always followed in the Gospels by the commission to preach. So it is to be with us. As one scholar puts it, "God's word of promise to us should become a proclaimed word of hope to others."[7] But such proclamation is impossible without empowerment; we will turn to that next week.

DAY FIVE

Digression: Theories People Use to Try to Disprove the Resurrection

You may find it interesting to pause briefly and consider some theories that people have put out in an attempt to explain away the events of Easter weekend by some other way than the rising of Jesus from the dead. You may be glad to know that there are no questions for you to answer today! But I hope that you will discuss the material. It is interesting that the skeptics do not deny the basic facts of Jesus' trial, crucifixion, burial and empty tomb; they just seek another explanation for them. Strange to say, it requires more faith—and more imagination—to believe in some of these theories than to believe in the resurrection.

> It is an embarrassing insight into human nature that the more fantastic the scenario, the more sensational the promotion it receives and the more intense the faddish interest it attracts. People who would never bother reading a responsible analysis of the traditions of how Jesus was crucified, died, was buried and rose from the dead are fascinated by the report of some "new insight" to the effect he was not crucified or did not die, especially if his subsequent career involved running off with Mary Magdalene to India. Whether sparked by a rationalism that seeks to debunk the miraculous or by the allure of the novel, often such modern imaginings reproduce ancient explanations that dismissed the death of Jesus on the cross, explaining it away through confusion or a plot.[8]

Let us look at a few of these theories, and the holes in them.

---

7. Bock, *Luke*, 3:1923.
8. Brown, *Death*, 2:1093.

#1: THE STOLEN-BODY THEORY

There are two versions of this theory. The first maintains that the disciples stole the body; this is the earliest attempt at explaining the resurrection away (see Matt 28:11–15). But there are several holes in it. Is it credible that disciples who fled when Jesus was arrested and hid while he was crucified would come out of hiding to steal his body when he was dead? And if they did show such courage, the guards would have prevented the theft (which was what they were there for!). Nor could the disciples have moved the stone and taken the body without disturbing the guards, if the guards were all asleep. And then there is the nature of conspiracies: most of them unravel quickly. If the disciples had plotted to steal Jesus' body, one of them would eventually have admitted it under the pressure of an investigation by the authorities. Would they really be prepared to die for something that they knew was a lie? Also, to foist such a lie upon the people would be contrary to Jesus' teaching, and to the disciples' own ethics as we know them. We may also note that grave robbing was considered very impious, which was one reason why it was a punishable by death. Also, grave robbers carried off goods. It was virtually unheard of for them to carry off a body. Above all, the idea that the disciples stole Jesus' body does not explain the appearances of the resurrected Jesus to the disciples.

Another version of this theory maintains that it was not the disciples who stole the body but the Jewish authorities, moving the body to another tomb for safekeeping. But why would they do themselves what they were afraid the disciples would do (see Matt. 27:64)? And if they had, why did they not explain what they had done and produce the body when the disciples began to preach the resurrection?

#2 THE WRONG-TOMB THEORY

This theory was first put about in 1907. It claims that the women who went to Jesus' tomb on Easter morning did not know where Jesus was buried, or got lost in the dark, and went not to Jesus' tomb but to another one, which happened to be empty. There they met a young man who said to them, "He is not here; see the place where they laid him" (apparently one is to imagine the young man pointing to another tomb). This ignores several things. First, it leaves out an important part of what the young man says in Mark 16:6. He does not say, "He is not here, he is over there;" he says, "He is not here; he is risen." Second, the Gospel

A Happy Beginning 133

narratives say that the women saw where Jesus was buried (Mark 15:47). Third, that the women should get lost in the dark is not impossible; but in only a few minutes it would have been light enough for them to realize their mistake. Fourth, this theory implies that the male disciples also went to the wrong tomb when they went to verify the women's story. Finally, if the disciples (women and men) had gone to the wrong tomb, the Jewish authorities would have been quick to point out the error and produce the body.

3 THE SWOON THEORY

This theory maintains that Jesus only seemed to be dead when he was taken down from the cross. He was then revived by the cold damp air of the tomb. He then climbed out of the grave clothes he had been tied into (and which were further weighed down by 75 lb./34.5 kg. of spices), broke the seal, pushed the stone away from the tomb entrance and fought off the guards (or moved the stone without attracting their attention), then walked naked and barefoot on nail-pieced feet through the streets of Jerusalem without being noticed. Some versions of this theory even have Jesus arranging this himself, by instructing Judas to betray him, taking a drug which would simulate death, and arranging for a doctor to hide in the tomb and care for him after he had been buried. But his plan was foiled when a Roman soldier stabbed him in the side, piercing his right lung and heart and killing him for real. All this strains credibility. And the idea that anyone could survive the mistreatment involved in crucifixion (we looked at the details of the process in Week 5) seems equally incredible. And then there is the reaction of the disciples. As Lee Strobel points out, "After suffering that horrible abuse, with all that catastrophic blood loss and trauma, he would have looked so pitiful that the disciples would never have hailed him as a victorious conqueror of death; they would have felt sorry for him and tried to nurse him back to health."[9]

#4 THE HALLUCINATION THEORY

This theory maintains that the resurrection appearances were hallucinations constructed in the imaginations of grief-stricken disciples. But this flies in the face of the psychodynamics of hallucination. Hallucination is a rare phenomenon, usually caused by drugs, mental illness or bodily deprivation. And those who hallucinate usually quickly realize that they are

9. *The Case For Easter*, 26.

hallucinating. Hallucination requires expectancy—and since the disciples were not expecting to see Jesus again (in spite of his predicting it), they would hardly imagine his presence with them. One may note also that the disciples included the hardheaded Peter, the skeptics Thomas and James, and the persecutor Paul—men scarcely likely to imagine things. And hallucination is an individual thing, that comes from the subconscious; it is impossible to control what someone else hallucinates. This also means that a group of people will not all hallucinate the same thing at the same time; and Jesus appeared to groups of people (whether a few people, the Twelve, or more than five hundred) more often than he did to individuals. The hallucination theory would require that over a period of several weeks, people of different backgrounds and temperaments imagined seeing the same person in various places. And if the disciples had imagined seeing the risen Jesus, his body would still be in the tomb, something that the Jewish authorities would be quick to point out.

#5 THE MYTH THEORY

This theory claims that the Easter story is patterned after the stories of dying and rising gods found in pagan religions. But there are several problems with this theory. First, many of these stories did not arise until after the New Testament was written—perhaps these pagan stories were patterned after the Easter story rather than the reverse. Second, most of these pagan stories take place in a mythological "once upon a time." By contrast, the death and resurrection of Jesus took place in history, in a definite time and place. Third, words like "resurrection" and "baptism," which originated in Christianity, are often not accurate when applied to paganism. These stories are not as close to the Easter story as using these words makes it appear. Finally, we must remember that Christianity has its roots in Jewish monotheism, which warns against mixing God's truth with other religions. "I am the LORD, and there is no other" (Isa 45:18). In the New Testament, Paul similarly warns Christians against mixing Christianity with paganism. "See to it that no one makes a prey of you by philosophy and empty deceit, according to the elemental spirits of the universe, and not according to Christ" (Col 2:8).

6 THE SPIRITUAL-RESURRECTION THEORY

This theory claims that the resurrection was a spiritual event, not a physical one. The body of Jesus decayed in the tomb like any other. But this disregards the fact of the empty tomb, which not even Christianity's opponents denied. And we have already seen that for Jews, the word "resurrection" implies the physicality of coming out of the tomb. And in Luke 24:39–43 Jesus proves that he is not a ghost. We may say that this theory lacks substance.

7 THE MUSLIM SUBSTITUTION THEORY

Islam sees Jesus as one of Allah's servants; it sees him as a prophet, but no more than that. The Qur'an says that a substitute was crucified in Jesus' place. This is similar to the Gnosticism which we discussed in Day One of last week. It is not certain what form of Christianity Mohammed came in contact with. There may have been Gnostics in Arabia in his time, so it is possible that he learned about Christianity from them rather than from orthodox Christians. Islam believes that Jesus ascended into heaven and is waiting there alive to return to earth at the end of time. There are two problems with this theory, a historical problem and a moral one.

The historical problem is that the Scriptures do not refer to the death of a substitute. In the Old Testament, it is the Messiah's death, not a substitute's, that is prophesied (Ps 22:16; Isa 53:5–10; Dan 9:26; Zech 13:7). In the New Testament, Jesus predicts his own death, not a substitute's (Mark 8:31; 9:12; 10:33–34; John 3:14; 8:28; 12:34). We may also point out something obvious—that if someone else had died in Jesus' place, Jesus could not have risen from the dead.

The other problem with the Muslim substitution theory is a moral one. Why would God allow an innocent substitute to suffer, especially if Jesus was going to ascend to heaven anyway? And why would God allow Jesus' family and disciples to go through the anguish of watching the crucifixion of a fake Jesus? (We should note that Islam reveres the mother of Jesus). "If the substitution theory were true, God would be directly responsible for one of the greatest deceptions in history."[10]

These are a few of the theories that have been put forward to explain the resurrection away as something other than the rising of Jesus from the dead. All of them have serious defects; none of them accounts for all the facts. The only explanation that does that is what the church has believed since its beginning—that Jesus did return from the dead.

---

10. McDowell and McDowell, *Evidence*, 212.

WEEK 8

Wind and Fire

DAY ONE

A Cloud, and Witnesses
Key verses: Acts 1:1–11; 2:1–41

THIS WEEK WE VISIT the book of Acts, which was written by Luke as Part 2 of his history of Jesus and the church. The book of Acts serves as a bridge between the Gospels and the letters of the New Testament. It provides a background for understanding the letters, especially Paul's. We may also say that the church has always called this book Acts of the Apostles, but in fact the apostles are not the main characters of the story. More than one scholar has suggested that the story is really about the continuing acts of Jesus through the Holy Spirit, as authorized and empowered by God.

Please read Acts 1:1–11, Luke's story of Jesus' final return to heaven. Verses 1–5 are an introduction which connects the book of Acts to the Gospel of Luke. In these verses Luke sums up Part 1 of his history and introduces Part 2. He dedicates this work to Theophilus, as he does his first one. Who Theophilus is we cannot say. The "most excellent" of Luke 1:3 may mean that he is a government official. The name means "one who loves God" or "beloved of God," but that does not mean that he is a symbolic figure and not a real man.

The disciples have gone to Galilee to meet the risen Jesus, as instructed. Having met him there several times, they have returned to Jerusalem. In verse 1 Luke says that in his first book he "dealt with all that Jesus began to do and teach." That he says "began" suggests that Jesus continues to work and teach through the church. This is an important theme in the book of Acts. The risen Jesus speaks to the disciples about the kingdom of God (verse 3; compare Luke 8:10; 12:32; 13:18–20). In other words, he continues the teaching that he gave them during his earthly life; he does not introduce some esoteric new teaching. This tells us that any teaching which claims to be a revelation from the risen Jesus will be consistent with Scripture. Jesus will not contradict himself by saying anything that is contrary to the written Word.

1. How is it significant that Jesus appears to the disciples over a period of *forty days* before his ascension?

Before his final return to heaven, the risen Jesus spends forty days with his disciples, preparing them for the next phase of what he has called them to do. This parallels his own experience, because he spends forty days in the wilderness, preparing for his ministry (Luke 4:2). We may also note that he returns "in the power of the Spirit" (Luke 4:14) and says, "The Spirit of the Lord is upon me" (Luke 4:18; he is applying Isa 61:1 to himself, verse 21). Similarly the Spirit comes upon the disciples at Pentecost. And it may not be a coincidence that just as Jesus and the disciples spend forty days preparing to receive the Spirit, so Moses spends forty days and nights on Mount Sinai preparing to receive the law (Exod 34:28; note that like Jesus, he fasts during this time). Forty days is also the time that the spies spend looking over the land of Canaan, which Israel is supposed to enter (Num 13:25). It is a period of time associated in Scripture with testing and preparation.

In verse 4 Jesus tells the disciples to wait in Jerusalem for what the Father has promised, namely the Holy Spirit (verse 5). Jesus has an assignment for them: "You shall be my witnesses in Jerusalem and in all Judea and to the end of the earth" (verse 8). But they cannot do this without the power which the Holy Sprit will provide. Like those first believers, we all have a call of God on our lives, whether it be to ministry, motherhood, or some other work outside the home. Like them, we must be empowered by the Holy Spirit before we can do what God has called us to do, and we may have to wait for that empowerment.

2. **Have you ever had to wait to be empowered by the Spirit before you could do what God had called you to do? If it is appropriate, why not share with the group?**

Verses 6–8 record the final meeting of the risen Jesus with his disciples. They ask him whether he will now restore the kingdom to Israel. In one sense, they are thinking politically; they think that now that he is crucified and risen, Jesus will lead them in an armed uprising against the Romans. But this is not what Jesus has in mind, any more than he did during his earthly ministry. In the Greek of verses 6–7, there is a contrast which does not show up in English versions. These verses could be translated, "they asked him . . . But he said to them . . ." Jesus redirects their focus: they are to witness for him, not play politics. In another sense, the contrast is between the disciples' focus on "when" and Jesus' focus on their mission. This is something that we must be aware of today. It is right for the church to look forward to Jesus' return in glory. But we must not allow anticipation to escalate into "second-coming fever" which speculates about dates, personalities, and details. These things are not for us to know. "But of that day or that hour no one knows, not even the angels in heaven, nor the Son, only the Father" (Mark 13:32). Besides, if Jesus' return is as imminent as some think it is, his disciples should not be sitting in a corner playing end-times guessing games. We should be reaching out to the world, so that as many people as possible are ready when Jesus does return.

We should also note that "witnesses" in verse 8 is a legal term. When witnesses testify in court, they testify to facts, not opinions. Disciples of Jesus will do best in their witnessing if they stick to the facts of what Jesus said and did, as recorded in Scripture, and of what God has done in their own lives (we looked at the importance of testimony last week).

Verses 9–11 are the account of Jesus' ascension to heaven. Jesus and the disciples are on the Mount of Olives (Acts 1:12). At the end of this last conversation, a cloud takes Jesus out of their sight as they look on. Not that this is the first time that the disciples—or at least, some of them—have seen Jesus in a cloud. Peter, James, and John saw this at the transfiguration (Luke 9:34). Earlier, Jesus has said that his opponents will see him "coming with the clouds of heaven" (Mark 14:62). And Paul assures the Thessalonians that all Christians, dead and alive, will be caught up in the clouds to meet Jesus in the air (1 Thess 4:17). In the Old Testament, clouds are a sign of God's glory. Exod 16:10 says that "the glory of the LORD appeared in the cloud." And when Moses finishes building the tabernacle, the cloud covers it, and God's glory fills it (Exod 40:34). So the fact that clouds are associated with God's glory and with Jesus' glory shows God's approval and vindication of Jesus.

For some time the disciples stand there, looking where Jesus has gone. Are they expecting him to return immediately? Are they simply amazed by what they have just seen? Whatever their reason for standing there, two men in white (presumably angels) appear with a mild rebuke. Just as they have just seen Jesus go to heaven in glory, so he will return in glory—but not immediately. Meanwhile there is work to do. They are to be witnesses for Jesus, continuing what he began. But while Jesus seldom left Israelite territory, his disciples will reach the entire world. They will be able to do this because the Holy Spirit will be operating in them with enabling power.

Jesus' ascension to heaven has paved the way for the coming of the Holy Spirit to empower the disciples for their work. This is why Jesus has told them earlier, "It is to your advantage that I go away, for if I do not go away, the Counselor will not come to you; but if I go, I will send him to you" (John 16:7–8). The church originates from God's initiative, not its own. We may also note that the Father, the Son, and the Spirit are all involved in founding the church.

DAY TWO

A Mighty Rushing Wind
Key verses: Acts 2:1–13

Please read Acts 2:1–13. The disciples are in Jerusalem, where they wait and pray rather than acting on their own initiative. On the day of Pentecost, they are all gathered in a house. This probably means the 120 people mentioned at Acts 1:15, which would presumably include the reconstituted Twelve (with Matthias replacing Judas, Acts 1:23–26); the women, including Jesus' mother; and Jesus' brothers, who have apparently come to believe in him since the incident of John 7:1–9.

Pentecost comes from the Greek word for *fiftieth*. The festival of Pentecost, also called the Feast of Weeks, was celebrated fifty days (a week of weeks) after the beginning of the grain harvest. On that day, at the end of the harvest, all male Israelites were to appear before the Lord at the temple to make an offering of thanksgiving for the harvest, and reflect upon their time of slavery in Egypt (Lev 23:15–21; Deut 16:9–12). Already in the Old Testament there is a connection between the blessing of the harvest and the blessing of the outpouring of the Spirit [see especially Joel 2, where God promises first abundant rain and an abundant harvest (verses 21–27), then the outpouring of the Spirit (verses 28–32, quoted by Peter at Pentecost)]. We may also say that just as in the Old Testament Pentecost is a harvest festival, so here in Acts 2 the harvest of souls begins (for the metaphor see also John 4:35–38).

In this regard we may note that the Greek word translated "had come" is a form of *pleroo*. As we saw in Week 5, this word is used of the fulfillment of Scripture. This hints that what happens is in fulfillment of Scripture, as Peter says later.

Luke begins his account of Pentecost by saying that the disciples are "all together in one place" (verse 1). The Greek word translated "together" in the RSV implies unity of mind. Those versions which say that the disciples are in one accord as well as in one place capture this idea properly. This is important; the Spirit cannot operate where Christians are divided. (Division seems to have been a problem in Corinth, 1 Cor 1:10–13). This is why Jesus, after teaching the disciples about the Spirit (John 14:16–17, 26; 15:26–27; 16:7–15), prays that the disciples will be one. This unity will be a witness for Jesus to the world (John 17:21–23). In Rom 15:5–6 Paul says that unity allows the church to glorify God. Before Pentecost they are disciples, but separate from Jesus. Once they are filled with the Holy Spirit, they are united to him and to each other.

In Eph 4:1–14 Paul says that Christian unity is an ingredient in spiritual maturity. He spends enough time on this subject that one wonders if division was not a problem in the church at Ephesus as well as in Corinth. This would not be a surprise. Ancient Greco-Roman society was very competitive, and it appears that this attitude of the world was getting into the church. Unity comes from the Spirit and leads to peace in the community (verses 3–4). The gifts that the Spirit gives are intended to build the church up, until believers reach unity and maturity, i.e., Christlikeness (verses 12–13).

3. How does this apply to us?

This principle applies to us today just as much as it applied to the early church. We must avoid competing in any way with our brothers and sisters in Christ. We must also avoid "majoring on the minors," allowing differences of opinion about small matters to become bigger than they should be, and cause division. If I like hymns and you prefer southern Gospel quartets, does that mean that we cannot work together as fellow-servants of God? (Music is a very important part of worship for me. But I recognize that others have the right to have tastes that are different from mine). Or perhaps I would like a blue carpet in the church building, while you would prefer a beige one. Does that really mean that one of us has to leave the church? I am not talking about major doctrinal issues—there are things that are important enough for us to take a stand on. But when we allow small things to divide us, it is the enemy who gets the advantage. "I appeal to you, brethren, to take note of those who create dissensions and difficulties, in opposition to the doctrine which you have been taught; avoid them" (Rom 16:17). "Have nothing to do with stupid, senseless controversies; you know that they breed quarrels" (2 Tim 2:23). "Avoid stupid controversies, genealogies, dissensions, and quarrels over the law, for they are unprofitable and futile. As for a man who is factious, after admonishing him once or twice, have nothing more to do with him, knowing that such a person is perverted and sinful; he is self-condemned" (Titus 3:9–11).

Let us return to the Pentecost narrative. The disciples are gathered together, waiting for God to act—and act he does. The house is filled with a sound like that of a rushing wind, tongues of fire appear above each disciple's head, and they are all filled with the Holy Spirit, which gives them the ability to speak in different languages. We may note, though we cannot discuss this issue fully, that this experience is shared by everyone present, both men and women. It is noteworthy that there is a sound (singular) of wind, and tongues (plural) of fire—this is a reflection of the one triune God. The wind is a symbol of the Spirit (John 3:8), the fire is a sign of God's presence (Exod 3:2; 13:21; 1 Kings 18:38; Ezek 1:13–14, 27). The word translated "utterance" at Acts 2:4 and the word translated "addressed" at Acts 2:14 are both from the same Greek word, *apophthen-*

geomai. This word refers to speech inspired by the Spirit; the tongues of verse 4 and Peter's speech are equally Spirit-given.

Because it is Pentecost, many Jews have come to Jerusalem from distant places, which are listed. Hearing the sound, a crowd of these pilgrims gathers. They are puzzled and amazed to hear the disciples—whom they regard as uneducated Galilean rustics—speaking the various languages of the people in the crowd. What catches their attention is not that these Galileans are praising God, but that they are doing it in the visitors' own languages. A complete discussion of the issue of speaking in tongues is not possible here, so I will just raise the following points. First, we must note that the disciples are speaking foreign, but earthly, languages. Second, the Spirit gives the disciples this ability for a specific purpose: so that people from other places will be able to understand the news of salvation in Christ. Third, this is a one-step phenomenon; there is no need for a second step of interpretation. All in all, this is a slightly different phenomenon from the two-step tongues-plus-interpretation, heavenly-language speaking in tongues which Paul discusses in 1 Cor 14. Finally, we should note that Luke spends less time on this sign than he does on Peter's speech which follows. This gives us a hint as to which is more important. One may perhaps compare 1 Cor 14:4–5, 19: "He who speaks in a tongue edifies himself, but he who prophesies edifies the church. Now I want you all to speak in tongues, but even more to prophesy. He who prophesies is greater than he who speaks in tongues, unless someone interprets, so that the church may be edified. . .in church I would rather speak five words with my mind, in order to instruct others, than ten thousand words in a tongue."

It is sometimes said that at Pentecost God reverses the judgment of the Tower of Babel, where people first begin to speak different languages (Gen 11:1–9). But that is not quite so. At Pentecost the crowd is not given the ability to understand the language spoken by the disciples; rather the disciples are given the ability to speak the many languages of the people in the crowd. We may say that at Babel God uses languages to thwart a human attempt to reach heaven by human means rather than God's way; at Pentecost God uses languages to proclaim not a human message but the message of the Gospel.

4. **What is not surprising about the people's reactions in verses 12–13?**

In verses 12–13 the crowd is divided. They wonder what the event which they have seen means. But some of them have already made up their minds: these people must be drunk (they do not seem to ask how wine would give the disciples the ability to speak foreign languages). In other words, some are confused, and some scoff. This is not surprising. Whenever there is a significant move of God, there will be people who scoff and try to explain it away. In Matt 12:22–32, for example, the people are amazed as Jesus casts out demons. They wonder if he could be the Son of David (i.e., the Messiah). But the Pharisees attribute his exorcisms to Beelzebul (a name for Satan). And we saw last week that people have been trying to explain away the resurrection of Jesus since that event happened. Today, schools, universities, and the media are full of attempts to explain God's activity in the world as the result of coincidence, imagination, or human effort. But we can be sure of this: "Toward the scorners he [God] is scornful, but to the humble he shows favor" (Prov 3:34).

DAY THREE

The First Christian Sermon
Key verses: Acts 2:14–28

Yesterday we looked at Pentecost, and saw the disciples filled with the Holy Spirit. This happens in a way that attracts a large crowd. If some scoff, some ask what this means; there is no reason to think that their question is not genuine. So Peter answers them. He does not reproach them for being perplexed; rather he sees an opportunity for witness. It is not surprising that it is Peter who speaks up, since he often acts as the disciples' spokesman during Jesus' ministry (see, e.g., Mark 8:29; 9:5; 10:28; 11:20; Matt 18:21). If he weakens on the night when Jesus is arrested, he has been restored and redeemed, and is ready to take the place of leadership to which Jesus has appointed him (John 21:15–17). He is able to speak so boldly because he is no longer relying on his own strength but on the Holy Spirit.

Peter, backed by the rest of the Twelve, stands up and answers the people. In ancient Judaism, sitting is the appropriate position for teaching, and standing is the appropriate position for preaching and prophesying. Peter begins by explaining what they have just seen, correcting the scoffers' misunderstanding before going further. In ancient Judaism, 9:00 A.M. was the hour for morning prayer, and it was customary to eat nothing before then; so it is unlikely that anyone would be drunk before then. Rather what is happening is to be explained as fulfillment of prophecy. Since wine was sometimes believed to enhance prophetic ability, it may be that the reader is supposed to think of Eph 5:18, "Do not get drunk with wine, for that is debauchery; but be filled with the Spirit." There the question is whether the Ephesians are going to allow themselves to be influenced by wine or by the Spirit. In Acts 2 the scoffers think that the disciples are under the influence of wine.

Having explained to the crowd what is not happening, Peter then begins to explain what is happening. The disciples are not under the influence of wine, but of the Spirit of God, and this is in fulfillment of prophecy. In verses 16-21 Peter quotes Joel 2:28-32. Previously the Spirit of God came upon a few people, chosen by God to meet a specific need. Now the Spirit is to be poured out on everyone, and the change is a sign that the end times have come.

5. What social boundaries does this outpouring of the Spirit cross?

The Spirit will be poured out on male ("sons . . . young men . . . old men . . . menservants") and female ("daughters . . . maidservants"), on young and old. Boundaries of gender and age are crossed. Both of these social boundaries were important in ancient Mediterranean culture. But there is another important social boundary which is not crossed here. That is the boundary of race: it is not said that the Spirit will be poured out on Jew and Gentile. That boundary will be crossed in due time, but the disciples are not ready for that yet. There are indications that when the time did come to cross that boundary, the church crossed it only with difficulty (see Acts 10:9–11:18; 15:1–30; Paul's own account of this last incident is in Gal 2:11–14).

The prophecy concludes in verses 19-21 with a warning of coming judgment (the signs mentioned were recognized as signs of the last days; compare Mark 13:24; 2 Pet 3:7, 10; Rev 6:12) and of the need to call on the Lord for salvation. But those who do call on the Lord will be saved. There do not seem to be any exceptions here. All those who call on the Lord will be saved—no one who calls on the Lord for salvation will be refused. In the original context of the prophecy in the book of Joel, "Lord" refers to God. But Peter will show that Jesus is Lord.

Peter then turns from the action of God through the Spirit in fulfillment of the written Word, to the action of God through Jesus, the Word made flesh. In verses 22–24 Peter says who Jesus is by summing up Jesus' ministry and Passion. The miracles that Jesus did show that he had God's approval (Peter reminds his hearers that they know what he is talking about, because they also saw what Jesus did). But although Jesus had God's approval, he was killed by human hands. "Lawless men" (verse 23) could refer to the Jewish leaders as well as the Romans. In Acts 4:27, it is said that both Jews and Gentiles opposed Jesus.

6. What is ironic about calling the Jewish leaders "lawless men"?

Israel's leaders prided themselves on knowing the law of Moses (John 7:49). Indeed Israel as a nation had long claimed that it was different from other nations because it had God's law. "He [God] declares his word to Jacob, his statutes and ordinances to Israel. He has not dealt thus with any other nation; they do not know his ordinances" (Ps 147:19-20). "In Judah God is known, his name is great in Israel. His abode has been established in Salem, his dwelling place in Zion" (Ps 76:1-2; compare also Ps 78:5-8). But knowing the law did not allow Israel's leaders to recognize Jesus when he came (John 5:39). And in joining with the Romans in opposing Jesus, Israel's leaders acted like people who did not know the law (on Day Three of Week 4 we saw how John links "the Jews" with the Romans as opponents of Jesus).

There is a contrast between the way that humans treated Jesus and the way that God treated him. Humans killed Jesus, but God raised him from the dead. Humans planned to destroy him, but God's "definite plan and foreknowledge" (verse 23) was the one that came about. That foreknowledge, however, does not lessen human responsibility ("You crucified and killed," verse 23). There is an interesting, and mysterious, interaction here between free human choice and the divine will and plan. God freed Jesus from death, because it was impossible for death to hold on to him. The word translated "pangs" in verse 24 refers to labor pains; death could not hold Jesus any more than a pregnant woman can hold a baby inside her body forever.

In verses 25–28 Peter explains why death could not hold Jesus. He does this with a second Scripture quotation, Ps 16:8-11, a Psalm of

David. In this Psalm David expresses confidence in, and gives thanks for, God's protection from enemies. Peter's meaning is that God gave Jesus the same protection that he gave David—protection from every enemy. In fact, God gave Jesus even more protection than David, because (as Peter will say later) David was not protected from death. This was so because Jesus was always sinless, and thus in proper relationship to God ("I saw the Lord always before me"). He did not rebel, so he could be confident that God would not leave him in death.

In this first half of his sermon Peter explains to the crowd that what they have seen is not drunken behavior but the outpouring of the Holy Spirit which was promised in Scripture. This action of God is made possible by the ministry, death, and resurrection of Jesus, whose miracles authenticated him as God's man. All this was foretold in Scripture. Now in the last days God is doing what was promised. Tomorrow, in the last half of Peter's sermon, we will see how God keeps that promise.

DAY FOUR

Both Lord and Christ
Key verses: Acts 2:29–41

Yesterday we looked at Acts 2:14–28, the first half of Peter's Pentecost sermon. The speaking in tongues inspired by the Holy Spirit has attracted a puzzled crowd. Peter explains where the phenomenon comes from, and that it is a sign of the end times, in fulfillment of prophecy. Jesus, Peter says, was God's man, and there are two things that prove this. First, God did signs and wonders through Jesus, as Peter's hearers know. Second, humans killed Jesus, but God raised him from the dead. This Peter also proves from Scripture, quoting part of Psalm 16, a Psalm of David.

Please read Acts 2:29–41. In verses 29–31 Peter justifies this interpretation of the quotation. David, he says, could not have been referring to himself in this Psalm, because he died and was buried (in the Passion narratives Jesus is linked with David; here he is contrasted with him). This his hearers know, because they know where David's tomb is (it was probably near the Pool of Siloam). The Jewish historian Josephus, writing at around the same time as Luke, says that in around 135 BC the high priest raided David's tomb, and later Herod tried to do the same, but the body was never disturbed. On the second occasion, a fire started and two men were killed. So Herod built the impressive memorial which Peter is talking about.

In verses 32–36 Peter turns from prophecy to Jesus' resurrection as fulfillment of that prophecy. Scripture shows that the Messiah will rise from the dead; Jesus rose from the dead; therefore Jesus is the Messiah. The outpouring of the Spirit which they see and hear is proof of the resurrection. Peter then moves to his third Scripture citation, which is Ps 110:1, an important verse in the early church. Many Jews of Jesus' day believed that this verse referred to the Messiah. This verse may have been important to the early church because Jesus himself used it to best the Jewish leaders in a debate (Mark 12:35–37; Matt 22:41–46; Luke 20:41–44). He is challenging them to rethink their expectations of who the Messiah would be. If the Messiah is to be the political Son of David, in what sense is he David's lord? He must be more than a political figure, and he is, because he will be seated at God's right hand. Here in Acts, Peter says that, as with Ps 16, David could not have said this about himself. Jesus' position at God's right hand, from which he gives the Spirit, in accordance with God's plan, indicates that God has vindicated him.

Peter then makes a final contrast between the way that humans treated Jesus and the way that God treated him. Humans killed him, but God has made him Lord and Christ. This is the heart of the message of Pentecost. Here *Lord* is a title of power and authority, which belongs to Jesus because of his incomparable character; *Christ*, the Greek equivalent of the Hebrew Messiah, is a title of deliverance and salvation, which belongs to Jesus because he has fulfilled all the prophets' hopes of a Redeemer who would atone for sin and restore humanity. The people's sin is that they have killed the one to whom God gave this unique position of Lord and Christ. That Peter says "made him" does not imply that Jesus was not Lord and Christ before his death and resurrection. In this regard we may note that Luke, who wrote Acts, begins his Gospel with the story of Jesus' miraculous birth.

7. Here Peter ends his sermon and leaves his hearers to react. What does this tell us about our own witnessing?

Several years ago, a lady who had been involved in church work for many years shared with me the First Rule of Preaching: "Stand up, speak up, and shut up." This is what Peter does here. He says what the Holy

Spirit gives him to say, then comes to an end. He gives his hearers an opportunity to think about what he has said, and the Spirit an opportunity to work. This is one reason why Peter gets the response that he does. We must remember this principle in our witnessing. We must say what the Holy Spirit gives us to say, and then leave the rest to the Spirit. We are eager to "get people saved," especially those whom we love, but that is the Spirit's job, not ours. Our job is to share the good news of salvation in Jesus, under the Spirit's guidance.

We may make a few more comments about this first-ever Christian sermon. First, we may note Peter's confidence and conviction about what he is saying. There are no *probably*'s or *I suppose*'s here. If what Peter has said about Jesus' life and death, and about the Scriptures, is true, then the resurrection was necessary, or God would have been violating his own principles. And the speech stresses that the work of Jesus and the giving of the Spirit are part of God's plan. As one scholar puts it, "Undergirding the salvation message is the united work of Father, Son and Spirit."[1]

In verses 37–41 is recorded the people's response to Peter's sermon. If Jesus really is the Messiah, they have brought guilt on themselves by the way that they treated him. Convicted of their sin, they ask what they should do. As one scholar puts it, "It was when Peter traced the story of this Man of Nazareth, crowned Lord of all, God's eternal Type, as well as God's perfect Redeemer, that these men cried out in the consciousness of their own sin."[2] The people are "cut to the heart" (the only time this expression appears in the New Testament) and ask, "What shall we do?" John the Baptist gets a similar response to his preaching (Luke 3:10, 12, 14). John replies in terms of ethics: they should share what they have; tax collectors (who were known for collecting as much as they could get, giving the Romans what they asked for, and keeping what was left over) should collect no more than what they are asked for; soldiers should refrain from violence and be satisfied with their wages. But Peter answers in terms of responding to Jesus. They must repent (that is the response) and be baptized (the outward sign showing the inward response), calling on Jesus as Mediator. If until now they have relied on obeying the law for salvation, they must now call on Jesus, because it is only through Jesus that they have access to God. By doing this they will receive the promise, that is, the Spirit, which is for them and their children, and for "all those

---

1. Bock, *Acts*, 137.
2. Morgan, *Acts*, 89.

whom the Lord our God calls" (verse 39). Here again we see a tension between free will (Peter urges them to repent) and predestination (the promise is for "those whom the Lord our God calls"). We may also note that repentance is mentioned before baptism, because it is repentance which brings salvation. Baptism is the public sign of that repentance.

Peter calls on the crowd to "Save yourselves from this crooked generation" (verse 40), which speaks again of coming judgment. The Greek word translated "save yourselves" in most English versions is better translated "be saved." There is no suggestion that they can do anything for their salvation except to avail themselves of what Jesus has already done for them. In response, three thousand people are saved. To put it another way, conviction (produced by the joint witness of man and Spirit) leads to enquiry, which leads to exhortation, which leads to obedience and addition. There may be a lesson here, that we cannot preach the good news of salvation without telling people that they need to be saved. Does Peter get such a response because he is so forthright?

I have talked about the response that Peter gets, but I am not suggesting that the response is solely the result of Peter's efforts. As Peter is led by the Holy Spirit in what he says, so the crowd is led by the Spirit in how they respond. That Luke says "there were added" in verse 41 means that it is God who is doing the adding (this is confirmed by verse 47). We must choose to believe, but we can only make that choice with the help of the Holy Spirit.

On that Pentecost the church was born in wind and fire. The tongues of flame that appeared that day have never gone out. May the same Spirit that inspired those earliest believers inspire us, their spiritual children.

DAY FIVE

Summary

And so we come to the end of our journey through the Passion story. We have struggled with Jesus through the night in Gethsemane while the disciples slept. We have watched as Jesus faced off one last time against his Jewish opponents, and while Peter and Judas stumbled. We have learned with Peter a painful lesson in humility, and from Judas about the danger of despair, and how sin, if it is not dealt with, will grow to destroy us. We have seen Pilate meet Jesus, and learned that it is impossible to be neutral about him. We have walked the Via Dolorosa and seen there the physical and spiritual agonies that Jesus suffered for our sake. We have seen Jesus dead and buried, and we have seen him, against all hope, risen from the dead. And we have been with the disciples at Pentecost and seen the church born in wind, fire, and the Holy Spirit. We also drew some important lessons for ourselves from these passages.

9. What is the significance of the fact that Calvary comes before Pentecost?

It is significant that Calvary comes before Pentecost, because we must have a crucified life before we can have the blessings that come with being filled with the Holy Spirit. What does it mean to live a crucified life? It means to take up one's cross, deny oneself, and follow Jesus. It means to set aside one's own desires and do God's will, as Jesus does in Gethsemane and at Calvary. Fleshly desires and sin hinder the Spirit's operation in our lives just as a vacuum cleaner cannot operate properly if its filter is clogged with dust. It loses its suction power. So also we lose our spiritual power if anything comes between us and God. Paul uses a different image to express the same idea when he says, "Do not put out the Spirit's fire" (1 Thess. 5:19 NIV). The image is that of quenching a fire by throwing water on it, which clearly would hinder the fire from doing its work. Fleshly desires and sin in our lives are like water which we throw on the fire of the Spirit. When we stumble into wrong attitudes or wrong behavior (which we all do sometimes) we must go to God so that he can clean the blockages away, and keep the fire from being quenched.

To live a crucified life is to crucify the flesh, to kill it instead of giving in to its desires. This is the only way that we can be free of its control and live by the Spirit. It is not too difficult to see that living by the Spirit, being controlled by the Spirit, is the only way to have the benefits that come with being filled with the Spirit. We who have made Jesus Lord of our lives have been united with him in his death. That means that we are dead to sin, free from its control. And just as he rose from the dead, we can walk in newness of life now, and will someday be united with him in resurrection (Rom 6:4–5).

Let us take a last look at some of the themes that have run through the passages which we have been studying. We saw:

- Jesus' resolute obedience. Once Jesus is certain of what God wants him to do, he does it, no matter what the cost to himself. He is the obedient Son who carries out his Father's will. He does not do this without fear and trembling, but he does not allow his emotions to stop him from completing the mission that the Father has given him. Facing his opponents, he does not hesitate to say what God wants him to say.

- The fulfillment of Scripture, and Jesus' prophecies. Everything that the Old Testament Scriptures say about the Messiah is true of Jesus. It was important to the early church to be able to show, especially to unbelieving Jews, that Jesus is the Messiah foretold by the Scriptures. We also saw that Jesus' own predictions about the events of his betrayal, arrest, death, and resurrection come true. Jesus is the Prophet whose prophecies are trustworthy because they are accurate. Jesus also makes predictions about events that are to take place after the end of the story. The reader, having seen that some of Jesus' prophecies come true, is encouraged to trust that those prophecies which have not yet been fulfilled will be fulfilled in due time. But there is more. If what God says in the Scriptures, and what Jesus says, comes about, that leads us to a third theme:

- God, or Jesus, is in control of events. Once Jesus is under arrest, his Jewish and Roman opponents may think that he is under their control. But they are not as in charge of events as they think they are. Everything that happens is in accordance with the divine plan. God's will is carried out by those who have no idea of the significance of what they are doing. The Jewish leaders believe that they are purging Israel of a heretic who is leading the people astray; the Roman soldiers who take Jesus to Calvary think that they are carrying out the routine execution of a would-be revolutionary. Both groups are unaware that they are co-operating in God's plan for the salvation of the world.

- David/Jesus parallels. We have seen throughout this study that Jesus, Son of David, is often compared with David. In the Passion narrative, Jesus is linked with David. Interestingly, Jesus is connected not with David the triumphant king, but with David in his time of weakness, distress, and opposition from enemies. In the Pentecost sermon of Acts 2, Jesus is contrasted with David, in that Jesus rose from the dead and is exalted at God's right hand, but David remains dead and buried in Jerusalem. This, Peter says, shows that David could not have been talking about himself in Ps 16 and Ps 110. He must have been talking about someone else, and the someone else that he was talking about is Jesus.

- Irony. This is really a literary technique rather than a theme. But we have seen plenty of it throughout the Passion narrative. In the Gospels and Acts, irony usually comes from the fact that the reader knows (or should know) something that the characters in the story do not. It is not inappropriate to use irony in telling the Passion story, because the biggest irony of all lies in the Passion story itself: "He [Jesus]. . .himself partook of the same nature [i.e., flesh and blood], that through death he might destroy him who has the power of death, that is, the devil, and deliver all those who through fear of death were subject to lifelong bondage" (Heb 2:14–15).

10. Of the material that we have studied over these past weeks, what has struck you the most vividly?

One thing that has struck me is how much Jesus went through, for my sake and yours. How can I doubt that I am loved and valued, when Jesus suffered so much to obtain my salvation for me?

I would like to conclude with the words of hymn writer George R. Woodward:[3]

> This joyful Eastertide,
> away with sin and sorrow!
> my love, the crucified,
> hath sprung to life this morrow.
>
> My flesh in hope shall rest,
> and for a season slumber,
> till trump from east to west
> shall wake the dead in number.

---

3. As in the *Cowley Carol Book*, 1902.

Death's flood hath lost his chill,
since Jesus crossed the river:
lover of souls, from ill
my passing soul deliver.

Had Christ, that once was slain,
ne'er burst his three-day prison,
our faith had been in vain,
but now hath Christ arisen,
arisen, arisen, arisen!

Bibliogaphy

Barclay, William. *The Plain Man Looks at the Lord's Prayer*. London/Glasgow: Collins, 1964.
Bauer, Walter, William F. Arndt, F. Wilbur Gingrich, and Frederick W. Danker. *A Greek-English Lexicon of the new Testament and Other Early Christian Literature*, 2nd edition. Chicago: University of Chicago Press, 1957, 1979.
Beasley-Murray, George R. *John*. WBC 36. Waco: Word, 1987.
Bock, Darrell L. *Luke*. Grand Rapids: Baker, 1994–1996.
Bock, Darrell L. *Acts* Grand Rapids: Baker Academic, 2007.
Brown, Raymond E., SS. *The Death of the Messiah: From Gethsemane to the Grave. A Commentary on the Passion Narratives of the Four Gospels*. 2 vols. New York/London: Doubleday, 1994.
Evans *Mark*. WBC 34B. Nashville: Thomas Nelson, 2001.
Gibson, Shimon. *The Final Days Of Jesus: the Archaeological Evidence*.New York: HarperOne, 2009.
Hagner, Donald F. *Matthew 14–28*. WBC 33B. Dallas: Word, 1995.
Hare, Douglas A.R.. *Matthew*. Louisville: John Knox, 1993.
Keener, Craig S. *A Commentary on the Gospel of Matthew*. Grand Rapids: Erdmans, 1999.
Kittel, Gerhard and G. Friedrich eds. *Theological Dictionary of the New Testament*, Grand Rapids: Eerdmans, 1964–74.
Liddell, H.G., and Robert Scott, ed. H.S. Jones. *An Intermediate Greek-English Lexicon*, Oxford: Clarendon Press, 1980.
McDowell, Josh, and Sean McDowell. *Evidence For the Resurrection*. Ventura, CA: Regal, 2009.
Moloney, Francis J., SDB. *The Gospel of Mark: A Commentary*. Peabody, MA: Hendrickson, 2002.
Moore, Beth. *Living Beyond Yourself: Exploring the Fruit of the Spirit*. Nashville: LifeWay, 1998.
Morgan, G. Campbell. *The Acts of the Apostles*. New York/Chicago: Revell, 1924.
Strobel, Lee. *The Case For Easter*. Grand Rapids: Zondervan, 1998, 2003.
Thayer, J.H. *A Greek-English Lexicon of the New Testament*, New York: Harper, 1892.
Vine, W.E., Merrill F. Unger, and William White, Jr., *Vine's Complete Expository Dictionary of Old and New Testament Words*, Nashville, TN: Thomas Nelson, 1996.
Wiersbe, Warren W. *Be Loyal: Following the King of Kings*. Colorado Springs: David C. Cook, 1980.
Wright, N.T. "The Resurrection of Jesus Christ—Part 1" *Haven Today* radio program originally broadcast March 24, 2008. Accessible at www.haventoday.org./bishop-nt-wright-resurrection-jesus-christ.p.1594.html.

www.ingramcontent.com/pod-product-compliance
Lightning Source LLC
Chambersburg PA
CBHW070943160426
43193CB00011B/1793